N O L A N

R Y A N

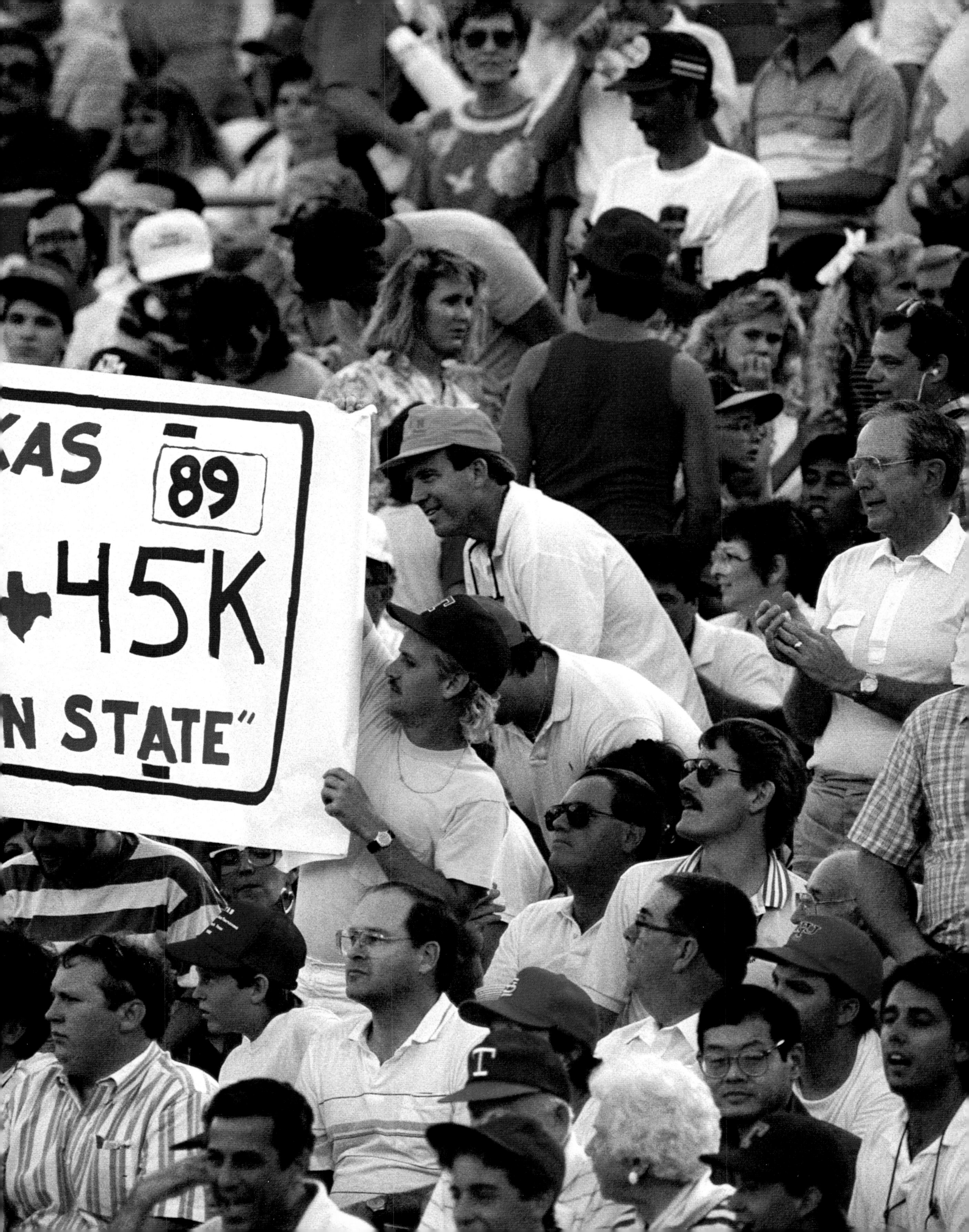
KAS
89
45K
N STATE"

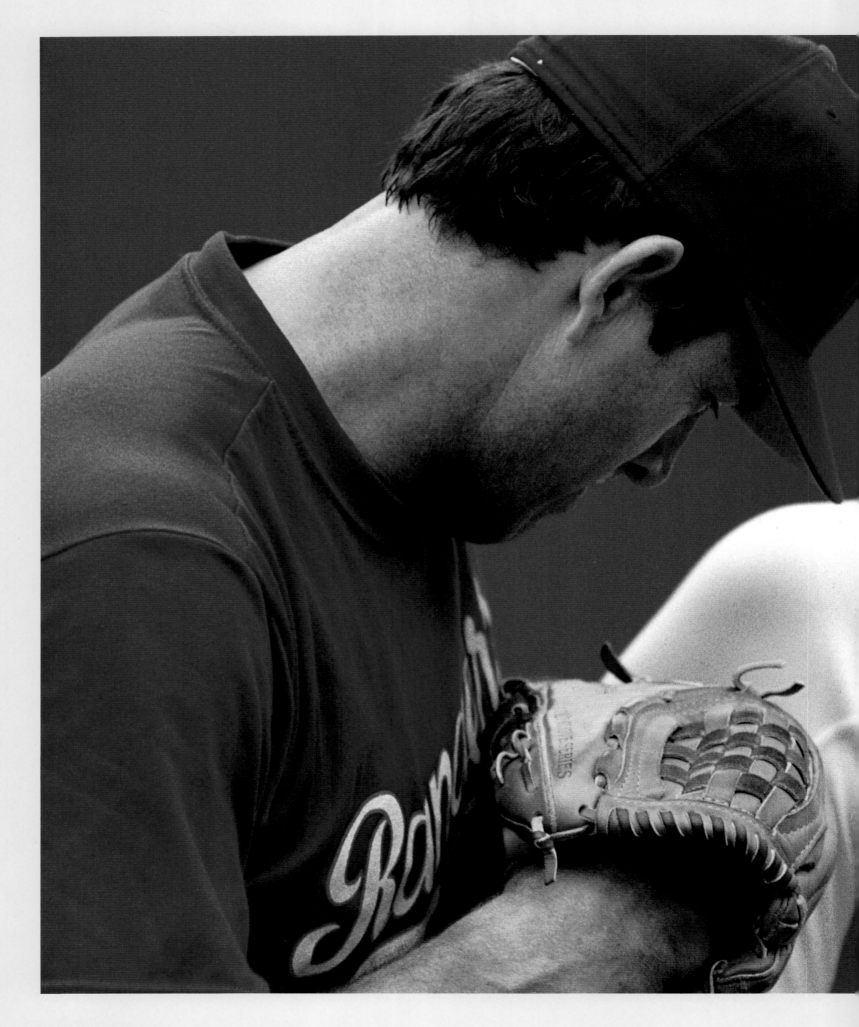

BRAD NEWTON

NOLAN RYAN

THE AUTHORIZED PICTORIAL HISTORY

CONTRIBUTING WRITERS

Jennifer Briggs, Fort Worth Star-Telegram
George W. Bush, Texas Rangers
Ron Fimrite, Sports Illustrated
Kenny Hand, The Houston Post
Marcy Kornreich, Boston Writer
Ron Kroichick, The Sacramento Bee
Jim Murray, Los Angeles Times
John Rawlings, The Sporting News
Jim Reeves, Fort Worth Star-Telegram
Tracy Ringolsby, The Dallas Morning News
Peter Schmuck, The Baltimore Sun
Mark Schramm, National Public Radio
Bill Shaikin, The (Riverside) Press-Enterprise
Arnie Stapleton, Dallas Sportswriter
Larry Swindell, Fort Worth Star-Telegram

SPECIAL PHOTOGRAPHY
TRUITT ROGERS

DESIGN
CHERYL CORBITT

THE SUMMIT GROUP
FORT WORTH, TEXAS

The Major League Baseball trademarks appearing on the cover and throughout the book were reproduced with permission from Major League Baseball Properties, Inc.

PUBLISHED BY

THE SUMMIT GROUP
1227 WEST MAGNOLIA
FORT WORTH, TEXAS 76104

Library of Congress Cataloging in Publication Data

Nolan Ryan: the authorized pictorial history / edited by D. Kent Pingel; contributing writers, Jennifer Briggs, George W. Bush, Kenny Hand, Marcy Kornreich, Ron Kroichick, Jim Murray, John Rawlings, Jim Reeves, Tracy Ringolsby, Peter Schmuck, Mark Schramm, Bill Shaikin, Arnie Stapleton, Larry Swindell
p. cm.

ISBN 0-09626219-7-8: $39.95.

1. Ryan, Nolan, 1947 – .
2. Baseball players – United States – Biography.

I. Pingel, D. Kent (Darrell Kent), 1960 – .
II. Briggs, Jennifer, 1961 – . III. Fimrite, Ron, 1931 – . IV. Hand, Kenny, 1949 – .
VI. Kornreich, Marcy, 1956 – . VII. Kroichick, Ron, 1965 – . VIII. Murray, Jim, 1919 – .
IX. Rawlings, John, 1951 – . X. Reeves, Jim, 1946 – .
XI. Ringolsby, Tracy, 1951 – . XII. Schmuck, Peter, 1955 – . XIII. Schramm, Mark, 1961 – .
XIV. Shaikin, Bill, 1963 – . XV. Stapleton, Arnie, 1964 – . XVI. Swindell, Larry, 1933 – .

GV865.R9N65 1991

796.357'092 – dc20
[B]

91-58019
CIP

Printed in Hong Kong

PRECEDING PAGES: COURTESY TEXAS RANGERS. ABOVE: BRAD NEWTON

I WILL NEVER FORGET THE NIGHT OF AUGUST 22, 1989, when Nolan Ryan struck out Rickey Henderson for his 5,000th strikeout.

It was a beautiful night. Our ballpark was full of energy because of more than 42,000 fans. My wife and twin daughters were with me as was the late Baseball Commissioner A. Bartlett Giamatti, who was watching what would turn out to be his last game.

Nolan needed five strikeouts when the night started to become the first man in history to reach that milestone of 5,000. Once he had four of those, the real drama began. On every two-strike pitch, thousands of camera flashes would fire as fans wanted to capture his achievement. We were witnessing a live version of the film, *The Natural*. When he threw a fastball by Rickey Henderson in the fifth inning for number 5,000, the response by the fans was unbelievable. Nolan received a thunderous ovation from the thousands who admired his baseball accomplishments as well as his personal style.

After the game, I congratulated Nolan for this great achievement and thanked him for his contributions to our game. His response was simple and direct: "We should have won the game."

Instead of focusing on his individual record, Nolan Ryan was concerned about a concept greater than self – in this case, his team.

For me, that response made the night of August 22, 1989 even more special.

GEORGE W. BUSH
MANAGING GENERAL PARTNER
TEXAS RANGERS

CONTENTS

"Folks seldom thought of Nolan and baseball in tandem. This kid's '56 Chevy, let alone his fastball, wouldn't go 95 miles per hour."

SUNRISE IN ALVIN: HINTS OF GLORY

NEAR THE TEXAS GULF COAST, where each summer morning drags in a new parade of hot and stagnant circumstances and kids hunt for catfish in nearby marshes infested with mosquitoes at best, sewer runoff at worst, Nolan Ryan took his first baby steps into a life only God himself could have predicted. From the day he was born in Refugio, Texas, January 31, 1947, there was never much indication he would throw anything professionally but the morning paper.

The sixth and final child of Lynn Nolan Ryan and Martha Lee Hancock Ryan took his father's name and his mother's diligence and began a steady, unassuming ascent to the sports world's equivalent of sainthood.

Nolan's dad wasn't a bank officer or a cattle baron. He was Mr. Ryan, who went to the red-brick Methodist church halfway across town and supported the family of eight as an oil-field supervisor, supplemented with money earned from a paper route. Mom wasn't an heiress or a civic leader. She was Mrs. Ryan, who always had the neighbor kids playing in her yard and who didn't want her youngest pulling catfish out of that nasty ol' bayou out back.

They were regular folks who always hated it when Nolan tied a long rope in the top of the cottonwood tree and swung out over the street, and they always stayed up worrying when he was late now and then.

· · · · · · · · J E N N I F E R   B R I G G S · · · · · · · ·

PRECEDING PAGES: ALVIN (TRUITT ROGERS), 1947 (COURTESY ALVIN MUSEUM SOCIETY)

The kids helped with Dad's paper route, and young Nolan was no exception. When an older brother graduated, Nolan began tossing the morning paper while in elementary school, going to sleep sometime after the sun went down and waking up a few hours before the day's milk bottles clanked against the gray cement front porch of the little beige house on Dezso Drive in Alvin,

One of Nolan's baby pictures
(COURTESY RUTH RYAN)

Texas, where the family moved six weeks after Nolan was born.

By all accounts he never complained about going without sleep or feeling drowsy as the American lit teacher read from the tales of Huck Finn or as English gave way to algebra and finally to baseball practice.

This matter-of-fact diligence is, perhaps, one of the only insights the world has on what made Nolan Ryan – a regular small-town kid who grew up on baked beans and ham, and cruised the Alvin Dairy Land for girls and soft-serve cones – one of the greatest ever to play the game of baseball.

THE SAME MAN who climbs back on the Exercycle for a late-night workout after each performance – even no-hitters – dutifully crawled out of bed each day as a child at 1 a.m. to roll the newspaper and toss it on the dusty, small-town doorsteps of Alvin.

Orange sherbet sunrise or sweaty Texas rain, Nolan's enthusiasm may have sagged privately, but his demonstrated devotion to getting things done never wavered.

This is not to say the kid who would become the King of Ks was all business.

Cowboys and Indians or cops and robbers were the biggest games in town, four decades before the kids of the '90s started playing "Nolan Ryan."

Nolan and his friend Jimmy Parker spent their days building rickety clubhouses with doors so small they fell apart when the boys went in and out on secret missions to the old rodeo grounds to sneak onto the bare backs of horses, or into the night to place a loaded line of Black Cat firecrackers on a sleeping neighbor's door.

The man with the golden arm was a child who almost always had a hand in some form of mischief, sneaking into the back door of the local theater or eating freshly trashed doughnuts in back of the bake shop.

Old neighbors like to recall the debacle of the calves.

The future rancher was raised in the city, but he always dreamed of raising livestock.

Worn out with this constant obsession, Mrs. Ryan and neighbor Jimmy Kirkendall's mom drove the boys into the nearby countryside to purchase two calves, which they carried home in the back seat of the station wagon.

They worried that their 11-year-old sons would get germs from the bottles the calves drank from,

Lynn Nolan Ryan Sr. and Martha Lee Ryan
(COURTESY RUTH RYAN)

and eventually the cows-to-be had to go because the mothers spent all their time sterilizing milk bottles.

CHILDHOOD AND TEEN-AGE triumphs didn't come only on the baseball field for Nolan. Winning, to Nolan, was being the proud 6-year-old who came home with a freshly snagged catfish, certain the one-pounder would feed a family of eight. It was pushing his '56 Chevy beyond its limits one teen-age spring at the beach on Galveston Island, and beating a bully with a '59 Plymouth.

It was bizarre accuracy in tossing the morning paper on the days the Chevy was plodding through the streets of Alvin. With a buddy riding shotgun and a stack of papers in between them, Nolan suggested that he could hit the streetlight with a paper. The toss from the left hand, which flew over the roof of the moving vehicle, hit the lamp.

The only thing peculiar anyone seems to remember about Nolan Ryan is his notable sense of sight. "He always noticed strange things," said one classmate.

A member of Nolan's graduating class recalled the night they were cruising Alvin in the Chevy and Nolan stopped conversation when he noted, in the slow, concerned drawl which defines most of his sentences, "Look at that water in that taillight up there."

The other kids could barely see the taillight on the car down the road. Nolan could see and take interest in the fact that it was half-way filled with water.

It was a life of simple pleasures for a boy of simple dreams.

Nolan, circa 1950 (COURTESY RUTH RYAN)

He wanted to marry Ruth Holdorff, raise kids in Alvin and hopefully, if he was really lucky, make the baseball team at a major university – or be a veterinarian.

A S HE WAS GROWING UP, folks seldom thought of Nolan and baseball in tandem. This kid's '56 Chevy, let alone his fastball, wouldn't go 95 miles per hour. And after all, everybody played Little League over at Schroeder Field, and he wasn't all that much better than the others.

Nolan wasn't a kid anyone re-members as a great Little-Leaguer, though he tossed one no-hitter while growing up and made the All-Star team as an 11- and 12-year-old. Mostly he remembers being good, just good, pitching in the hot gray flannel uniforms which defined the dugouts of the 1950s. His teams never won any championships. In fact, they never even advanced that far in tournament play, Nolan recalls.

There was nothing in his pitching delivery – one developed mostly by throwing rocks at turtles and water moccasins in the bayou – to suggest he would become one of the greatest ever to play the game of baseball, al-though his pitching was significantly

wilder than his peers', to the point that some kids were afraid to bat against him.

Eleven-year-old Ronnie Jinks was, perhaps, the first person ever hit by a Nolan Ryan pitch. Ronnie went to bed early that night nursing a sore shoulder. Nolan was so upset that his mother fed him two aspirin and sent him to bed.

Alvin High's 1965 "Most Handsome" (COURTESY RUTH RYAN)

Coaches recall that the young pitcher's arm began to develop velocity during his sophomore year in high school, when he realized that maybe he couldn't throw harder than anyone else, but he could throw farther, once tossing a softball 309 feet.

By the time he graduated from Alvin High School in 1965, baseball had become his vocation.

But when he signed with the Mets that year, not even his proud high school coaches would have suggested that in just a few years, he would pitch in a World Series. And, barring a late-inning pitch from Nostradamus, they certainly wouldn't have guessed that almost 30 years after he peeled off his last orange Alvin game jersey, he would toss his seventh big-league no-hitter.

For the humble kid from Alvin, raising three kids and a few calves would have been enough.

The First Ballfield.
This diamond in the rough,
a vacant lot next to the
Ryan home on Adoue Street,
was at one time a field too
exclusive for Nolan.
Reportedly, older children in
the neighborhood would
play, leaving Nolan on the
side, glove in hand, waiting
for his big break.

Mrs. Ryan and Nolan's
siblings Mary Lou, Bob,
Judy and Jean, from back
left, pose with a camera-shy
Nolan after a rare snowfall
in Alvin, circa 1950.

Nolan whizzes by as next-door
neighbors Jim and Bob Macdonald
meet outside their house on Adoue
Street to prepare for an Alvin
Redbirds Little League game.

The neighborhood gang demonstrates Alvin "mass transit" as Nolan takes the reins of a donkey headed down Adoue Street, 1953. The riders include Nolan, Barbara Macdonald, Judy Ryan, Jean Ryan and Shannon Hicks. Bobby Carlisle was "stood up" on this ride. (COURTESY JIM AND BOB MACDONALD)

Barbara Macdonald, Jim Macdonald and Nolan pose in front of a more popular mode of transportation, the '52 Chevy from which Nolan and his father threw papers.

(COURTESY JIM AND BOB MACDONALD)

11

The corner of Sealy and Gordon, where Nolan and his father bundled The Houston Post *every morning.* (TRUITT PHOTOGRAPHICS)

Schroeder Field, site of the first no-hitter, Alvin Little League. (TRUITT PHOTOGRAPHICS)

Nolan's first All-Star appearance, Alvin Little League. (COURTESY RUTH RYAN)

The high school has annexed the primary school building and a new elementary school has been constructed since the days when Nolan spent time on the mound and under the hoop. But things haven't changed much in Alvin since this shot was taken of the Alvin Independent School District, circa 1956. The Yellowjacket gym is visible in the upper left quadrant of the photo and the baseball diamond can be seen at the lower right.

(COURTESY ALVIN MUSEUM SOCIETY)

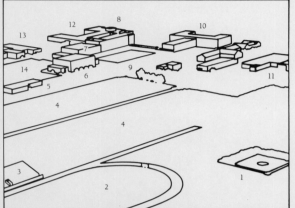

Key to Photo Description

1 Baseball Field
2 Football Field
3 Home Bleachers
4 Athletic Practice Fields
5 Agriculture Building
6 High School Boys' Gym
7 High School Girls' Gym
8 High School Auditorium
9 Tennis Courts
10 Main High School Building
11 Cafeteria and Student Union
12 Junior High School
13 Elementary School
14 Elementary Playground

The '65 Jackets. *First row: Charles Thomas, Dennis Mathis, Bobby Jacobs, Donald Brown, Larry Huffman, Darrel Hunt, Eddie Allen, Pat Wagner and Billy Childress. Second row: Coach Jim Watson, Don Methvin, Ronnie Nelson, Jimmy Waters, Butch Decuire, George Pugh, Nolan Ryan, Jerry Spinks and Donald Ault, captain.* (COURTESY RUTH RYAN)

A scene from an Alvin High game, 1965. The Yellowjackets won district and regional championships, advancing to the state finals.
(COURTESY RUTH RYAN)

In 1965, Nolan received the Outstanding Athlete Award and the Tinnin Cup at Alvin High School. The Tinnin Cup was awarded to a boy or girl who met the following requirements: The student did not drink or smoke, was passing at least 75 percent of his/her schoolwork and was a junior or senior participating in at least two sports programs at Alvin High. (COURTESY RUTH RYAN)

1965 All-State Pitcher Nolan Ryan with a record of 19-3. (COURTESY RUTH RYAN)

Insets: As the story goes, when Ronnie Jinks, left, was 11 years old, he was the first person pegged by a Nolan Ryan pitch. Jinks is shown here in his Alvin High School senior picture. Right: Nolan's high school coach, Jim Watson, who once said, "My only claim to fame with Nolan is that I kept him in shape, didn't hurt his arm and made sure he was ready to go. I also taught him a mental toughness that has never left him." (COURTESY RUTH RYAN)

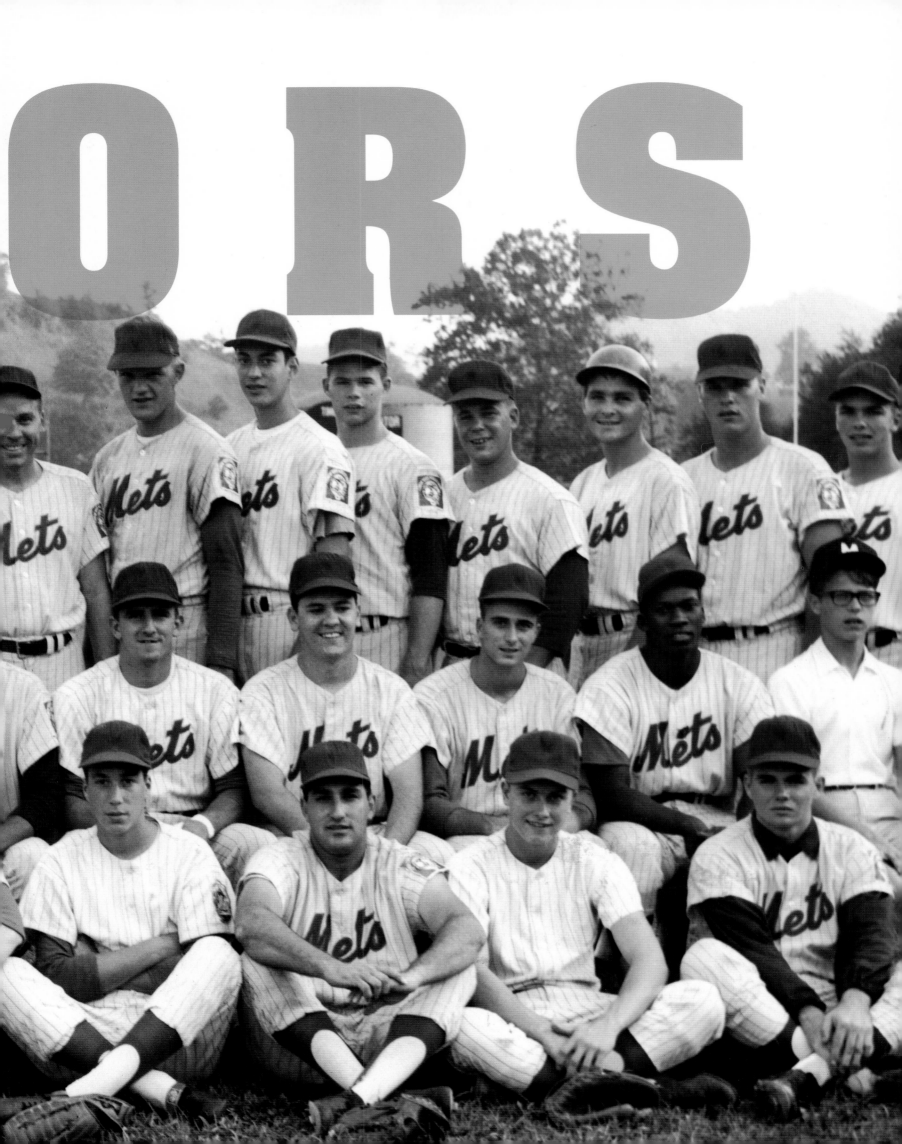

"I wanted to
shout it out to the
world, what I had
found, but I had
to keep this kid
top secret."

RED MURFF

SCOUT FOR THE NEW YORK METS

**Minor Leagues
1965-1967
21 Wins
10 Losses**

1965
• Signed by the
Mets in the
eighth round
of the draft
• July: Arrived
in Marion to
begin minor-
league career
• Topped the
Appalachian
League in hit
batters (8)

1966
• Selected as
Western
Carolinas'
Pitcher of
the Year,
Greenville
• Led the league
in wins (17)
• Led the league
in strikeouts
(272)

1967
• Missed most
of the season
due to a six-
month military
obligation and
elbow trouble
from an arm
injury in
Jacksonville,
Florida

1968
• Recuperated
and joined the
Mets in New
York, ending
his minor-
league career

TOURS OF DUTY: MINORS & MILITARY

NOLAN RYAN WALKED AWAY FROM A NO-HITTER ONCE, but he had a pretty good reason. It happened on a muggy September afternoon in the fifth inning of a Double A Eastern League game in Williamsport, Pennsylvania. Though untouchable, Ryan only had been scheduled to pitch four innings. Manager Bill Virdon asked him if he wanted to stay in and go for the no-hitter, but Ryan had other things on his mind.

"I told him, 'If it's all right with you, Mr. Virdon, I'd just as soon move along to New York City,' " recalls Ryan. "You know, a no-hitter in the minor leagues doesn't really mean anything."

So Ryan caught a cab and headed to the airport. Hours later, he was standing nervously in the clubhouse at Shea Stadium while they fitted him for a Mets uniform. The year was 1966, and baseball would never be the same.

It had been a whirlwind 14 months for the 19-year-old from Alvin, Texas, a small ranching and farming community near Houston, known back then for not much of anything.

But it had begun three years before when, on a whim, Mets scout Red Murff stopped by Clear Creek High School, where Alvin High was playing in a tournament. What Murff saw that day sent his heart into overdrive. "I was almost

A R N I E   S T A P L E T O N

holding my breath," says Murff, "because I couldn't believe it."

Here was a tall, lanky 16-year-old sophomore, with a penchant for the basketball hoops, taking the mound and throwing the ball harder than anyone Murff had ever seen.

Ryan's high school coach, Jim Watson, filled in Murff, telling him about the kid's wildness, about how  Ryan's heaters would break the bones of catchers, about how some opponents refused to bat against him . . . . "I wanted to shout it out to the world, what I had found," says Murff. "But I had to keep this kid top secret."

M URFF FOLLOWED Ryan's blazing fastballs for a year and then sent this report to the Mets: "Skinny, right-handed junior. Has the best arm I've seen in my life. Could be a real power pitcher someday."

That is, if Murff could persuade Ryan to sign.

Murff had assured Ryan that he'd be a high pick in the draft. But on the one day Murff's boss, Bing Devine, flew down to see this wonder kid, Ryan was spent. Watson, angry over two straight 1-0 losses, had made the team run several miles the previous afternoon. Then he made them face Ryan's fastballs for 30 minutes of batting practice.

"Jim told me that Ryan couldn't pitch because he had run him till he puked," Murff says. "But I told him he had to throw Nolan. It was the only time Devine would be down." Ryan didn't make it past the third inning and left trailing 7-0. But it didn't shake Murff's confidence in him, and the Mets took Murff at his word.

The Mets wound up drafting Ryan in the eighth round in 1965. He was the 295th player taken in the draft. Ryan wasn't sure about signing, but his father told him it was the right thing to do. So Ryan, who would become baseball's first $1-million player, signed for the tidy sum of $500 a month.

"When he signed that night," remembers Murff, "I took him aside and I said, 'Nolan, if you become as good as you think you can, and you're half as good as I think you are, one day you'll make so much money that we'll both be embarrassed to talk about it.' "

But Ryan wasn't so sure.

"I had no idea if I'd ever make it to the major leagues, if I had what it took," says Ryan.

I N THE MINORS, Ryan had some very good times, like when he struck out 19 batters in a nineinning game against Pawtucket in Single-A ball in 1966.

THE SPORTING NEWS

He also went through some very bad times, like when he hurt his arm a year later and missed much of the season before a full recovery landed him in the majors for good at the start of the 1968 campaign.

"As far as my minor-league career," says Ryan, "I can't really say that I accomplished anything as far as learning to pitch. You see, in those days they didn't have pitching coaches at the minor-league level. The only reason I excelled down there was that I was blessed with a lot of ability to throw the baseball.

"And I threw as hard as I could for as long as I could, and because of my natural ability, I moved up the ladder. So, when I got to the major-league level, I really didn't know how to pitch. I was just gifted with a great arm."

After signing in 1965, Ryan reported to Marion, Virginia, in the Appalachian Rookie League, where he went 3-6 with 115 strikeouts in 78 innings. In Marion, he learned firsthand about homesick evenings, long bus rides and showers without hot water.

A year later, Ryan went 17-2 with a 2.51 earned run average and 272 strikeouts in 183 innings at Greenville, South Carolina, in the Single A Western Carolinas League. He was promoted to Williamsport, where he went 0-2, but had 35 strikeouts in 19 innings before his two-game stint with the Mets, where he was 0-1 with six strikeouts in three innings.

Ryan left the team on September 20 to start his courses at Alvin Community College. He was thinking about spending time with his high school sweetheart, Ruth. History and English would take up some of his attention, but mostly he was feeling pretty good about baseball, which was now paying $600 a month.

"I finally started to believe that maybe I could compete at the big-league level," recalls Ryan. "Then, when I was in school that year, I got my draft notice."

Ryan immediately called the Mets, who urged him to sign up for a six-year commitment in the Army Reserve rather than take a two-year tour in the regular Army. Six years in the Reserve would mean sporadic starts during his developmental years, but Ryan had little choice. "You look at the alternative," Ryan says. "The alternative was going to Vietnam." It could have been two years between starts, "or worse."

Ryan missed much of the '67 season because of his six-month military obligation. "When I came out, the Mets sent me down to Florida to get in shape, and I hurt my arm in Jacksonville and didn't pitch anymore that whole year," Ryan says.

B UT 1967 wasn't all bad. That was the year Nolan and Ruth got married.

"Ruth is as strong as Nolan," says Murff. "They make a strong family. I went to their wedding and asked Nolie if he was going to South America to rehabilitate during the winter, and she took his arm and said she wasn't going to let him get away anymore. But I told her, 'Nolan Ryan doesn't belong to me or to you. He doesn't belong to Alvin. Or to Texas. Or to the United States. He belongs to the world.'

"Years later, she told me that she was mad at me for a long time because of what I said, but that now she understood what I was talking about."

In fact, Ruth talked Nolan out of retiring a couple of times in his early years with the Mets, when he was having a difficult time finding his control and a good delivery.

"She deserves as much of the credit for my career as anyone," Ryan says. "She really helped me out during some tough times in my career. I got so frustrated over my control problems that at times I was just ready to go ahead and pursue something else."

Ryan recuperated so well after the '67 season that he would never see the minors again. His date with destiny had begun, although New York took some getting used to.

"That was the biggest adjustment, going to New York," Ryan says. "I

had never lived in a big city before. Going to Marion, Virginia, and Greenville, South Carolina, I don't believe there's any culture shock. I can't say there's a whole lot of difference in those towns."

But, as evidenced by his long and storied career, Ryan adjusted quite well to

1966
Williamsport

1966
New York

1965
Marion

1966
Greenville

1967
Jacksonville

1967
Winter Haven

THE MINORS

N.Y. Mets

PAIGE MENEFEE

life in the big leagues. He perfected his delivery and control, and developed a cutting curveball that's faster than most pitchers' fastballs. He also added a circle-change to go with his blazing fastballs and got better with age.

"He's a miracle," says Murff. "Nolan Ryan is the best example of what a major-league baseball player is supposed to be.

"Thank God we found him."

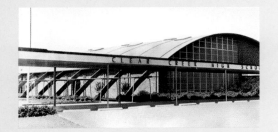

A stunning pitcher from Alvin
High School faced the charges of
Clear Creek High School in a
1963 Texas high school show-
down. Red Murff was in the
stands, his eyes bulging. The
rest is history.

Talent scout Red Murff's keen
eyes, endless footwork and
negotiating prowess accounted for
many of the talented players who
signed with the Mets during their
heyday, including the '69 World
Champions.

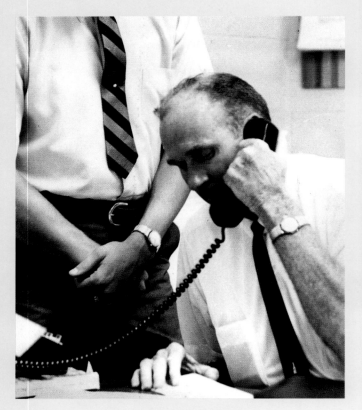

Men of Foresight.

Bing Devine, New York Mets president, gathered his talent scouts in January 1967 for this shot taken in St. Louis. Devine is seated second from the right. The list of visionaries includes, seated from left: Charley Frey; Ken Boyer, Mets third baseman; Walter Millies; Paul Tretich; Ollie Vanek; Devine and Joe McDonald. Standing, from left, are Mimi Alongi; Whitey Herzog; Red Murff; Herschel Martin; Roy Slavers, minor-league manager; and Russ Sehon.

(UPI/BETTMANN)

In July 1965, a lanky Texan standing 6 feet, 2 inches and weighing about 150 pounds shuffled off a bus in Marion, Virginia. Hanging at his side was what would become one of the greatest arms in baseball. His throwing arm was strong but young and ever so wild. The president of Marion Baseball Inc., Robert Garnett, above, met Nolan at the Greyhound bus stop. Garnett says he carried the pitcher's bags because he thought the young man might "break in two." Garnett drove Nolan to Wytheville, Virginia, to join his new team on the road. The first time Nolan pitched was when the squad returned to Marion.

"I shall never forget that his first pitch, a fastball, knocked the catcher's mitt off," Garnett says. "He had the opposing team so scared that they were ducking coming out of the dugout."

(COURTESY ROBERT S. GARNETT)

Among Garnett's memories and collectibles is this baseball signed by the Marion Mets.

The '65 Mets.

The Marion Mets, vintage 1965, finished third, behind Salem and Wytheville, in the Appalachian League. The Mets attracted 29,868 spectators that year, partially fueled by the fireballer from Alvin. Nolan's 4.38 ERA ranked fifth in the league among pitchers who threw for 70 innings or more. The '65 Mets, from front left, were: Curt Brown, Mickey Walker, Tom Garrett, Bill Strong, Mike Arsenuk, Bill Vinci, Ed Boggs and Connie Garnett. Second row: James Plummer, Roger Whitlock, Dale Del Bello, Dave Brasier, Nolan Ryan, Dave Hayes, Ron Burchfield, Donny Carmichael, Jim Ursillo, Frank Pickens and Woody Linkous. Back row: Gary Strom, Tom Davis, Bill Collins, Steve Renko, Jim Bibby, Pete Pavlick, Larry Wallin, Greg Arsenuk, Fred Rheam, Jerry Bark, Lou Williams, Ken Williamson and Carl Nicholsen.

(COURTESY ROBERT S. GARNETT)

In the '60s, minor-league players reportedly were shuffled around most sporadically. Players would come and go, sometimes having been signed for only a day – simply to prevent another team from signing a talent. Other times they were called up to "the bigs." This 1965 shot shows Marion minor-league hopefuls Bob Johnston, Roger Harrington and Nolan Ryan. (COURTESY RUTH RYAN)

The '66 Mets. *The Greenville Mets and Williamsport, two clubs in the New York Mets farm system, shared Nolan in 1966. (Notice that the player standing fourth from the left wears a cap from another club, probably the Marion Mets.) With Williamsport, in the Double A Eastern League, Nolan's batting average was .167, and his ERA was a slim 0.95 with 35 strikeouts in 19 innings. The Williamsport squad finished in fourth place. Greenville, in the Single A Western Carolinas League, finished second. Nolan posted a .132 batting average and an ERA of 2.51. Nolan's pitching statistics were the fourth best in the Western Carolinas League.*

(COURTESY RUTH RYAN)

People say Nolan hasn't changed much over the years. He goes out of his way to help other people today, just as he did in 1965 when he and Marion Mets teammates autographed this bat and presented it to David Roland, a sick child who was unable to attend "bat night" at the ballpark. Time has taken its toll on many of the signatures, but Nolan's name is clearly visible.

(COURTESY DON ROLAND)

Nolan poses with "Spike" Kelly, a former boxer and ironworker – one of the most avid fans of the Jacksonville Suns. As word of Nolan's fastball spread, more than 2,500 Jacksonville fans turned out for a game when Nolan was scheduled to pitch. As he warmed up for the game, something snapped in Nolan's elbow, and he was unable to throw. Promoters offered refunds to the crowd, but only four tickets were returned. (COURTESY RUTH RYAN)

In this sequence, the camera illustrates Nolan's windup and delivery in 1967. Compared with shots taken 20 years later, it seems apparent that the young pitcher's power depended on the arm alone, rather than the strength of the legs, as demonstrated in Nolan's now-characteristic knee-to-the-chest windup.

(SERIES COURTESY FLORIDA TIMES-UNION)

"...when I came up, we had Koosman and, soon after that, Gentry. Those were great young arms. But you looked at Nolan, and you saw there was something extra no one else had."

TOM SEAVER

NEW YORK METS

ASCENT TO THE BIGS

I N 1964, THE WOEFUL NEW YORK METS won 53 games and lost 109. They also signed two talented young pitchers, Jerry Koosman and Frank McGraw.

In 1965, they were worse: 50-112. They signed Jim McAndrew, Jim Bibby and a gangly right-hander from tiny Alvin, Texas, Lynn Nolan Ryan. In 1966, they broke the 60-victory barrier for the first time. They signed Danny Frisella and a bona fide collegiate pitching star, Tom Seaver.

In 1967, they lagged, winning only 61 games. They signed two more pitchers, Gary Gentry and Jon Matlack.

Suddenly, this was a team with a future. "We had pitching, boy. We knew we had pitching," says Whitey Herzog, the team's director of player development during those years. "We just didn't know we had *him*."

They were hard throwers, every one. And all of baseball could see that this precocious team was rich in baseball's most important commodity. Experts loved to guess which one would be the brightest star. Seaver was poised and precise. Koosman was the wicked left-hander. McGraw boasted a strange nickname, "Tug," and an even stranger pitch, the screwball. Gentry and Bibby offered raw power. Even so, *him* means only one man: Ryan.

"I don't remember our first encounter," says Seaver, who undoubtedly will join the Hall of Fame in 1992, his first year of eligibility, "but it didn't take long

· · · · · · · J O H N   R A W L I N G S · · · · · · · ·

New York Mets
1968-1971
29 Wins
37 Losses

1968
• April 14: Won first major-league game by defeating the Houston Astros

1969
• April 29: Recorded first official save in Mets' history, against the Montreal Expos

1970
• April 18: Set a New York club record with 15 strikeouts against the Philadelphia Phillies

1971
• December: Traded to the California Angels for Jim Fregosi after finishing the season at 10-14

to see that this was somebody special.

"You have to understand, when I came up, we had Koosman and, soon after that, Gentry. Those were great young arms. But you looked at Nolan, and you saw there was something extra that nobody else had.

"We all thought we had great fastballs. But his . . .

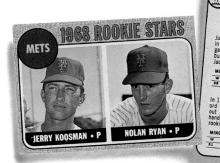

he had that extra pop that nobody else had."

Despite the praise, the adulation and the near-cult following that developed around the Texan, Nolan Ryan *the legend* far exceeded Nolan Ryan *the pitcher* during seven seasons in the Mets organization. Management always saw potential. It infrequently saw the pitcher. "How could they know how good I'd be?" Ryan himself says. "I didn't even have a clue."

Ryan burst to attention in 1966, with Greenville, South Carolina, in the Class A Western Carolinas League. He had been selected by the Mets in the 1965 free-agent draft – the first time the draft had been used, as a way to equalize talent throughout baseball – but not until their 12th pick.

"I was young and a little wild," Ryan says. "I didn't always know where the ball was going."

After a rapid climb up the minor-league ladder, it was on to the Mets near the end of the '66 season.

"We started him in a game in the Astrodome," Herzog recalls, so the hometown fans could see their hero-in-the-making. "He wasn't really ready. He was wilder than a March hare. But, my God he could throw."

The Mets caught only a glimpse of what Ryan would become, and that game stood as a haunting symbol for his up-and-down career in New York: One inning he pitched (he was lifted for a pinch-hitter in the second inning) four hits, four earned runs, two walks and one wild pitch. Oh yes, he struck out the side.

THE NEXT SEASON was practically wiped out by Ryan's U.S. Army Reserve duty and his first arm injury. He pitched only 11 innings, but he recorded 23 strike-outs. In fact, of the first 20 outs he got for Jacksonville, Florida (Class AAA), 17 were strikeouts.

Despite the disappointment of 1967, he broke into the Mets' rotation the next season. Again, the Mets saw tantalizing potential. Ryan arrived late to spring training because

of his Army duty, and he struggled. Finally, Manager Gil Hodges told Ryan he would get one last start in the spring to earn a spot on the roster. He faced the St. Louis Cardinals on March 26 and made his case. He pitched four innings and struck out six, including Orlando Cepeda, Johnny Edwards and Mike Shannon in succession. Cepeda called Ryan "the best young pitcher I have seen since I came into the league."

RYAN BECAME one of the three new faces in the rotation, along with Koosman and Dick Selma. They joined Seaver to form one of the hardest-throwing staffs in baseball. Hodges gave Ryan his first start of the season at the Astrodome, and Ryan responded.

He fanned the side – Ron Davis, Joe Morgan and Hal King – in the bottom of the first and chalked up seven strikeouts in the first three innings. He had a no-hitter for five and ended up giving up three hits in 6 ²/₃ innings while gaining his first major-league victory.

"Is he fast?" Astros cleanup hitter Rusty Staub was asked after the game. "For the first five innings he was as fast as anyone in the game. Fast as [Cincinnati's] Gary Nolan was last year."

He continued to be fast. Pitching coach Rube Walker, a man with a long drawl but a quick wit, liked to say Ryan's pitches "had some hurry on 'em."

He set a team record with 14 strikeouts in a 3-2 victory over Cincinnati. After six starts, he led the league with 58 strikeouts in 44 innings, but he tailed off soon after. Some of Ryan's figures were impressive – a 3.09 ERA and 133 strikeouts in 134 innings – but he spent a month on the disabled list due to a recurring problem with a blister on the second finger of his right hand, and he had to take time out for his reserve duty. He had only a 6-9 record, and both interruptions would foreshadow continuing problems in New York.

The blister resulted from a childhood injury and became quite celebrated in the press. "I was trying to get the top off a coffee can, using one of those openers, and I cut my thumb, second and third fingers," Ryan remembers. Scar tissue formed, and then the friction from throwing the ball across the seams would make a nasty blood blister.

"Gus Mauch [the Mets' trainer] tried all sorts of stuff to fix it, including having me dip my finger in pickle brine. That seemed to work for a while, but it came back. Then there was the time away for the reserve duty."

Hodges, a stern and quiet leader, encouraged Ryan but was never a public cheerleader. His praise was always reserved, somehow qualified. It was couched in terms of what

Ryan "could be . . . when he learns to get the ball down."

Ryan is not sure what his manager thought of him that year or any other, for that matter. "Gil was a little intimidating for the younger guys," Ryan says. "He was a stern man, not real outgoing. He wasn't mean, but we never had a close relationship."

The next three seasons were a succession of highs and lows.

The '69 season was a storybook for the Mets but a lamentable chapter for Ryan. He was in and out of the rotation, with 10 starts and 15 relief appearances. He struck out 92, but he logged only 89 innings. He fought a pulled groin muscle early in the season, and it finally put him on the disabled list for a month. Then there was a month lost to reserve duty.

W HEN THE National League Championship Series ended in a 3-0 wipeout of the Atlanta Braves, Ryan had only one relief appearance to show for it. But he made it count. He pitched seven innings in relief of Gentry, giving up only three hits and striking out seven in the game that vaulted the Mets into their first World Series.

The Series was more of the same. The rotation remained Seaver, Koosman and Gentry. Ryan made an appearance, again in relief of Gentry, and earned a save in Game Three.

"Was I disappointed not getting to start? No, I couldn't expect to," Ryan says in retrospect. "I really hadn't been in the rotation all year. I was really up and down with my control. I was inconsistent."

The next season was even more of the same. There was the brilliant beginning (15 strikeouts in a one-hit victory, then a two-hit loss and a three-hit victory), but a deep descent. The death of his  father in mid-season was a difficult blow. He finished 7-11 with 125 strikeouts in 132 innings.

Finally, '71 appeared to be the year Ryan would bloom. He started on a tear, going 6-1 with a 1.08 ERA in the first two months. "For the first time in my life, I can't wait for my next start," he said at the time. Had he arrived? "At the end of the season, if I'm 20-5 or 18-6, then I'll say it. I've had too many ups and downs to be sure I've arrived."

The season ended at something a good deal less. He won only four more games and finished at 10-14. He struck out 137 in 152 innings, but his walks soared to 116, his career high in the majors to that point. Hodges lost patience.

"I had the military obligation the whole time I was in New York," Ryan says. "Pitching is all in consistency, and I was never able to get that. I'd be gone during the season . . . and missed some weekends. It was hard, especially for a power pitcher."

Nor was Ryan particularly comfortable living in New York. He worried about his wife, Ruth, when the team was on the road, and the lifestyle, in general, was a far cry from Alvin. "It was a completely different kind of life than I knew," Ryan says. "I can't say I ever adjusted to it."

Herzog offers another view. "Probably the worst thing that ever happened to Nolan Ryan was the Mets' winning

the Series in '69. We were still a few years away from having a good club, but after you win once in New York, people expect you to win all the time.

"We never had great offense, and Gil was afraid Nolan would never have enough control to win a lot of

games 2-1 or 3-2. We were pitching-rich, and Gil wanted to make a deal. That's why Ryan got traded."

The year ended with the first real blow to Ryan's career. In December of 1971, he was part of a trade that brought shortstop Jim Fregosi to New York from the California Angels. California also received pitcher Don Rose, catcher Francisco Estrada and outfielder Leroy Stanton in the swap.

"A bad deal?" Herzog says. "Bob Scheffing [the Mets' general manager] called me and asked me to call Stanton and tell him he had been traded. I didn't think Stanton for Fregosi was a good deal. I didn't even know about Ryan. It might be the worst deal in history."

Harry Dalton, the Angels' general manager, confessed years later that Ryan was not even his first choice of pitchers. "I asked for Gary Gentry first, but Bob said Gentry was not available. We knew Ryan was wild and his control problems hadn't improved, but he had that sensational arm. He was worth a shot. We knew the Mets' pitching was good enough that we could get somebody, maybe McAndrew or Matlack if not Ryan."

Seaver is still puzzled by the move. "He wasn't even close to having the physical and mental maturity that he would soon develop," Seaver says. "From a player's standpoint, he was a guy you looked at and you said, 'Just a matter of time.' He was like Sandy Koufax, only the Dodgers were smart enough to keep Koufax."

Ryan was stung at the time, but it turned out to be the best thing that could happen. "Anytime you're traded, it hurts," he says. "It means somebody thinks you couldn't do the job.

"Looking back, it's the biggest break I ever got. I knew I was going to a team where I would be in the rotation, and they were going to let their young players have time to grow."

COULD RYAN have become the greatest strikeout pitcher in history and an absolute lock for the Hall of Fame if he had stayed with the Mets? "It's hard to say I would . . . or wouldn't," he says. "But the pressure to win there was terrific. You come back to the question of would they be patient enough."

The Angels, of course, were patient and prescient. "I've seen him at every step," says Herzog. "What he's accomplished, well, it's impossible to imagine."

An attentive pitcher from Alvin, Texas absorbs the instruction of pitching coach Harvey Haddix, a "southpaw."
(COURTESY RUTH RYAN)

1968 Mets Roster: *Front row – Gus Mauch, trainer; Joe Pignatano, coach; Rube Walker, coach; Yogi Berra, coach; Eddie Yost, coach; Joe Deer, assistant coach. Second row – Al Weiss; Cleon Jones; Gil Hodges; Jerry Grote; Gary Gentry; Rod Gaspar; Duffy Dyer. Third Row – Jim McAndrew; Rommie Agee; Cal Koonce; Ken Boswell; Tom Seaver; Jerry Koosman; Ron Swoboda; Wayne Garrett; Kevin Collins; Leo Niss, traveling secretary. Back row – Bob Sanchez, equipment manager; J.C. Martin; Ron Taylor; Ed Kranepool; Don Cardwell; Donn Clendenon; Nolan Ryan; Art Shamsky; Les Rohr and Nick Torman.* (COURTESY RUTH RYAN)

"Everyone" was talking about the Mets' young pitcher, Nolan Ryan, according to news stories from 1968. This sequence shows Nolan pitching against the Los Angeles Dodgers in Shea Stadium. Nolan was tagged with a 3-2 loss on the day, although he struck out 11 Dodgers before he was relieved in the eighth inning.

(AP/WIDE WORLD PHOTOS)

Pitching coach Rube Walker helps to lay the foundation for a pitching career that eventually would tower above the competitors.

(THE SPORTING NEWS)

*A young, red-hot Nolan Ryan poses
with one of the balls he used to fan 14
Cincinnati batters, May 14, 1968.*

(UPI/BETTMANN)

*The Mets first introduced Nolan to the
healing power of pickle brine to combat
the blisters that have plagued his
throwing fingers throughout his career.
This 1968 shot, left, is one of many
featuring the remedy.* (AP/WIDE WORLD
PHOTOS) *Even Life magazine dedicated
two photos and a forced rhyme to
Nolan's brine time, May 31, 1968.*

(LIFE, COURTESY COLLECTOR LARRY CERNOCH)

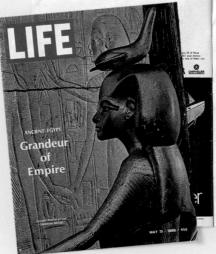
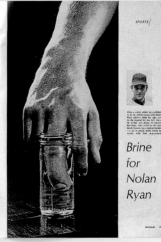

An ever-stoic Nolan accepts the congratulations of Mets Manager Gil Hodges, pitching coach Rube Walker and peer Gary Gentry after a successful 1968 outing.
(COURTESY RUTH RYAN)

A casual Nolan enjoys a little bubble gum and his loafers after a hard day "at the office."
(COURTESY RUTH RYAN)

Jerry Koosman and Tom Seaver listen as Nolan shares a little Alvin insight, 1968. (COURTESY RUTH RYAN)

National League Pennant Game. *Nolan fires a strike during the Mets'*
National League triumph over the Atlanta Braves, October 6, 1969. The Mets
won the game 7-4. Nolan, relieving in the third and final game of the 1969
National League pennant race, cinched the victory, hurling the 8-year-old
Mets into their first World Series. (UPI/BETTMANN)

In the sequence above, Nolan looks stunned as he records the victory, then lets out a Texas-size holler as catcher Jerry Grote flies toward him. The two Texans unite in a "victory two-step" and then head for the dressing room.

(Following page) Friend and fellow pitcher Tom Seaver jumps up and joins in the celebration.

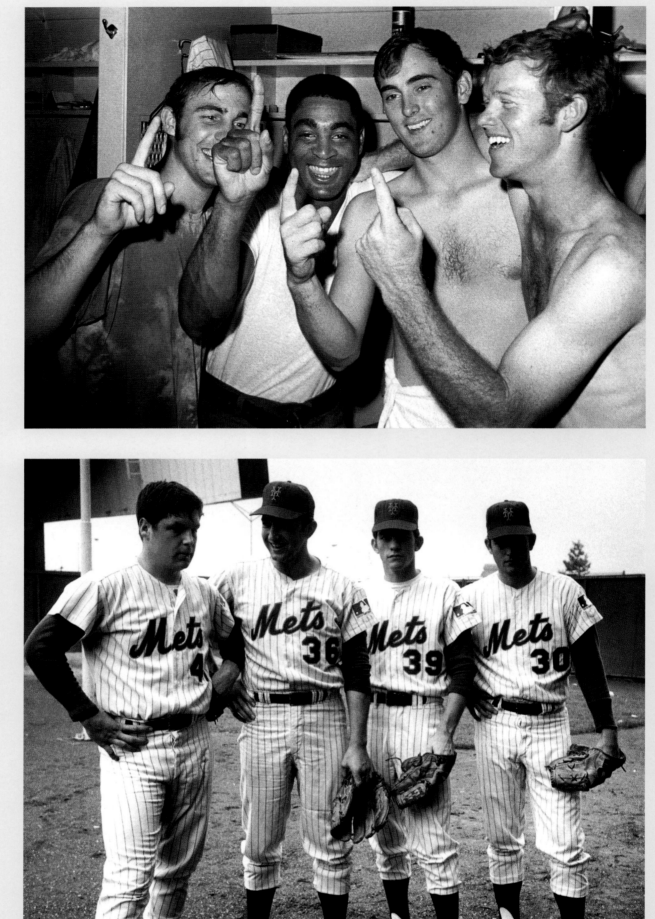

Ken Boswell, Tommie Agee,
Nolan and Wayne Garrett
continue the celebration in
the locker room. (UPI/BETTMANN)

Tom Seaver, Jerry Koosman,
Gary Gentry and Nolan
pose after a bullpen workout
in preparation for the World
Series. (UPI/BETTMANN)

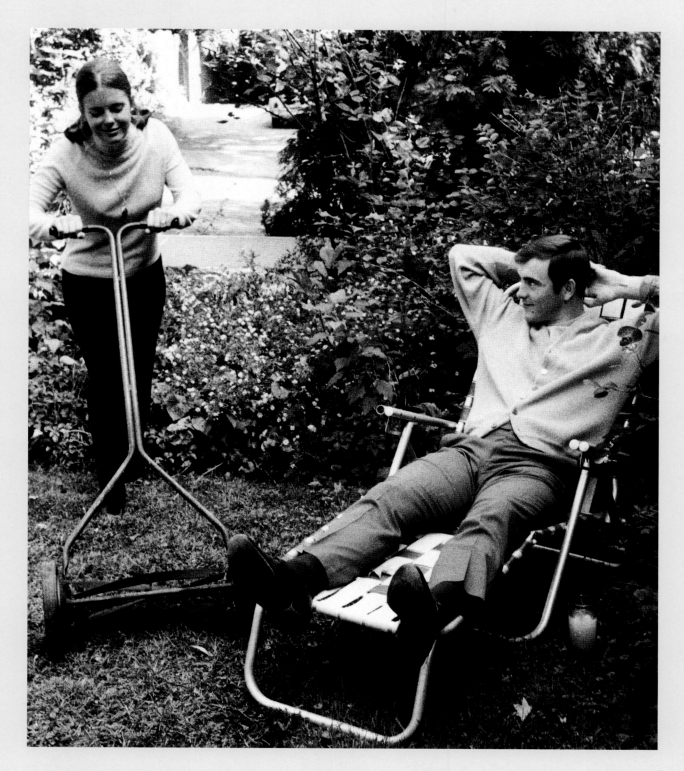

*The day after the Mets'
triumph over the Atlanta
Braves, Nolan Ryan's wife,
Ruth, steps in as relief
gardener. She told Nolan to
relax and save his energy
for pitching so that he
might enjoy a long and
successful career.*

(UPI/BETTMANN)

Game Three. *One of Nolan's contributions to Game Three of the World Series, October 14, 1969.*

(UPI/BETTMANN)

Mets center fielder Tommie Agee dives and gloves Paul Blair's fly ball for the third out in the seventh inning of Game Three. The bases were loaded with Orioles before the catch ended the threat. Art Shamsky backs up the play as three of the 50,000 spectators look on.

(AP/WIDE WORLD PHOTOS)

Nolan accepts congratulations after recording a save in Game Three of the Series. The Mets blanked the Orioles, 5-0. Gary Gentry claimed the victory, lasting through 6⅔ innings for the Mets.

(WALTER IOOSS JR./SPORTS ILLUSTRATED)

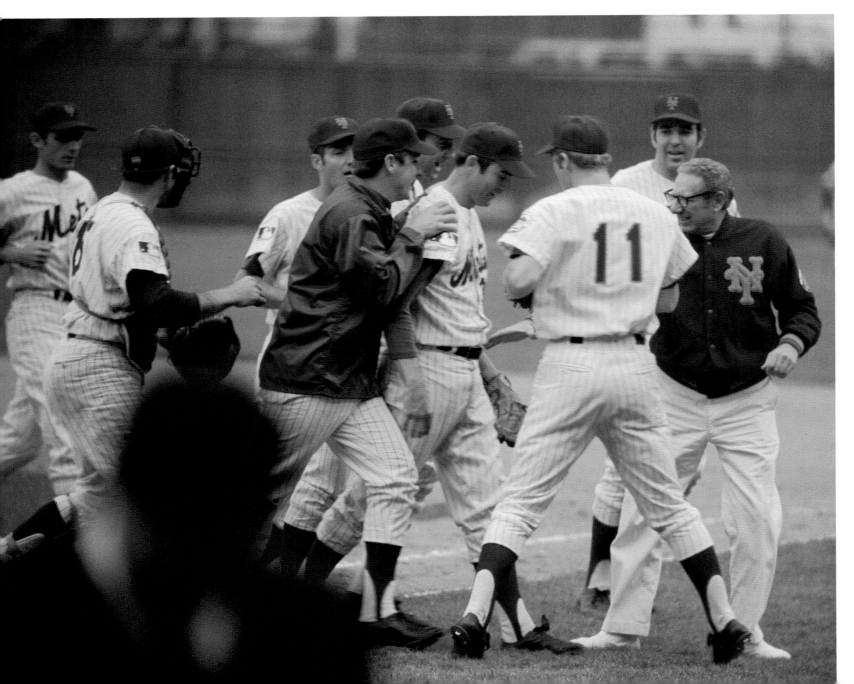

Game Five of the World Series. *Outfielder Ron Swoboda drives a double down the left-field line, scoring Rod Gaspar from second and putting the Mets ahead in the eighth inning of the fifth game. Gaspar was running for Cleon Jones, who opened the bottom of the eighth with a double.*

(AP/WIDE WORLD PHOTOS)

Jerry Koosman and Jerry Grote start the celebration as the Mets become world champions. Koosman went the distance in the 5-3 win. (WALTER IOOSS JR./SPORTS ILLUSTRATED)

The champions charge Koosman as he leaves the mound.

(WALTER IOOSS JR./SPORTS ILLUSTRATED)

The camaraderie and team-
work that ended in a victor-
ious autumn began with
spring fever. Nolan enjoys a
little "Tom foolery" with
teammates Seaver, Tug
McGraw and Danny Frisella
as they douse coach Joe
Pignatano. (UPI/BETTMANN)

(Left) Confetti and ticker
tape fill the concrete canyons
of Manhattan as news of the
miracle spreads. (ERIC
SCHWEIKARDT/SPORTS ILLUSTRATED)

IT was the worst trade in 115 major-league seasons. Nolan Ryan's performance · · · · · · · · · · · · · · · subsequent to the transaction made it that.

On December 10, 1971, the game's off-season Hot Stove League was captivated by a blockbuster five-player deal, consummated during the six-week period in which inter-league trading was permissible. The National League's New York Mets sent pitchers Nolan Ryan and Don Rose, catcher Francisco Estrada and outfielder Leroy Stanton to the California Angels of the American League, in exchange for Jim Fregosi.

Four for one. Fregosi was a shortstop, but it was no secret that the Mets were obtaining him to play third base.

In the headline news of national sport, it was "the Fregosi trade." He was the big name, although Nolan Ryan, at that early juncture in his long career, was anything but a nobody.

The trade signified that the Mets had given up on Ryan – that they were apparently convinced the lean young right-hander would never master control while he was a fireballer.

And a fireballer he certainly was. At the raw age of 19, he made two late-season relief appearances for the Mets in 1966, striking out six in three innings. He was compared to Bob Feller, a youthful phenom of three decades earlier; and as with Feller, Ryan's early career was hampered by a proclivity for walking too many batters.

The Mets farmed him out in '67 but brought him back the next year for what would take on the appearance of a four-year tryout. He was the major league's hardest-throwing right-hander, against whom opposing batters could manage only six hits per nine innings. He fanned almost a batter an inning, but bases-on-balls too often were his undoing.

In those four seasons combined, he pitched only 507 innings, winning 29 decisions while dropping 37. That included a 6-3 mark in the "Miracle Mets'" pennant-winning 1969 season, when Ryan also started and won a game in the champion-ship playoff series. There followed a single World Series appearance that was a microcosm of Nolan Ryan at that time: two and one-third innings in relief, yielding one hit, no runs, three strikeouts, two walks.

He was etched as a future star, but also was posed as a poor contrast to Tom Seaver, the Mets' superlative right-hander who threw almost as hard as Ryan while exhibiting consistently brilliant control. The Mets' management became impatient with Ryan, but not so impatient as were New York fans or the local press corps.

Favored to repeat as National League champions in 1970, the Mets finished third, then fell another notch to fourth in '71. Ryan followed with a 7-11 record in '70 and a 10-14 accounting the next year, and New York baseball writers decided to make him the whipping boy for the team's wholesale disappointments.

He had been an "untouchable," but after the '71 campaign the Mets were shopping him, finding no takers after their insistence on a star player in return.

MEANWHILE, those New York writers expressed another chronic grievance. From the franchise's ludicrous beginning in 1962, the Mets encountered annual difficulty at third base.

After the 1971 season the Mets, pressured relentlessly by the writers, resumed their annual habit of scouring both leagues in search of a representative third baseman. Within their own league they courted the Montreal Expos' Bob (Beetle) Bailey and Houston's Doug (Red Rooster) Rader. But neither Expos nor Astros were tempted by the bait: left-handed pitcher Jerry Koosman, a Series hero two years earlier but a fallen star, at least briefly, with a 6-11 slate in '71.

The four-for-Fregosi trade was the brainstorm of Mets Manager Gil Hodges (who would die on the eve of the '72 season), thinking that Fregosi, a shortstop who had lost a step, could give the Mets a good show at third base. But they knew that Fregosi wouldn't come cheap.

And he didn't. The Mets prepared a package that included Koosman, right-handed pitching prospect Don Rose, in whom the Angels were mysteriously interested, catching prospect Francisco Estrada and veteran second baseman Ken Boswell. The Angels almost accepted the proposition, but at a late hour proposed that the right-handed Nolan Ryan replace Koosman in the Mets' provision.

Mets General Manager Bob Scheffing was reluctant to part with Ryan, but Whitey Herzog advised him to snare Fregosi at any cost. Herzog then was the Mets' director of player development – the position he would leave in 1973 to take his first managerial job, with the Texas Rangers. Scheffing's judgment was that if the Angels got Ryan, they couldn't have Ken Boswell. The Angels countered with a request for Leroy Stanton, which Herzog probably okayed. Outfielder Stanton had enjoyed a monster 1971 season for Tidewater, the Mets' Triple-A affiliate.

They shook hands and signed the papers. It was a deal. Ryan, Stanton, Rose and Estrada for Fregosi. Unconfirmed reports had the Mets sweetening the kitty with cash estimated from $100,000 to $350,000.

A ND IT WAS baseball's worst trade ever.

Not the best trade. The worst one.

And surely that requires some explanation.

In the classic sense, a good baseball trade is one that benefits both teams involved. A poor trade is one that quickly is proved inequitable.

A good trade may be a one-for-one, as in 1947 when the Yankees swapped star second sacker Joe (Flash) Gordon to the Cleveland Indians for ace right-hander Allie (Chief) Reynolds. Yankee pitching was solidified by the addition of Reynolds, generally considered number one on a famous staff that led the New Yorkers to six pennants and Series conquests in the next seven seasons. But the addition of Gordon made Cleveland competitive, and helped secure for the Indians the 1948 flag and subsequent world championship – the only year the Yankees did *not* win.

The famous one-for-one trade of right-hander Rick Wise (from the Phillies to the Cardinals) for left-hander Steve Carlton certainly wasn't a good trade, but it also wasn't bad, because, although Carlton scaled peaks of greatness in Philadelphia, Wise was a good-to-excellent pitcher for many years thereafter. A truly bad one-for-one was the Detroit Tigers' delivery of young left-handed pitching star Billy Pierce to the

Jim Fregosi

(AP/WIDE WORLD PHOTOS)

Chicago White Sox in trade for veteran catcher Aaron Robinson, who soon faded from the scene, while Pierce glittered another 17 years.

Oh yes, there were some others.

In mid-1964, the Chicago Cubs sent superstar-to-be Lou Brock, along with nondescript hurlers Paul Toth and Jack Spring, to the Cardinals for bygone stars Bobby Shantz and Ernie Broglio and journeyman outfielder Doug Clemens. A three-for-three terrible trade.

In 1982, the Phillies and Cubs swapped shortstops – veteran star Larry Bowa for Ivan DeJesus, younger and promising. Within a few years it acquired the character of a very bad trade indeed, because an almost anonymous rookie second baseman accompanied Bowa to Chicago as a throw-in. He was Ryne Sandberg, who has gone on to win an MVP award, a home run title, and eight consecutive Gold Gloves, and may be the game's closest approach to perfection in a present-day position player. Yet the Phillies' 1982 indiscretion can't be called a truly bad trade, simply because DeJesus shortstopped the Phillies to a league championship in 1983, even if he wasn't very good afterward.

Two factors made the Mets-Angels deal of late 1971 the worst ever: the utter failure of Jim Fregosi in a New

York uniform and the superlative performance of Nolan Ryan from the moment he became a California Angel.

In fairness to Fregosi, he had never played third base before. He was a six-time All-Star shortstop in the American League, recognized as the Angels' outstanding player over the team's first decade. (In contrast to the hapless Mets, the Angels were an astonishingly successful franchise team, finishing third in only their second year.)

Fregosi's American League bat had some pop, with a high of 22 home runs, and he brought a career average of .268 to the Mets. Where he was a bust: Besides proving an insecure third sacker in 85 games there in '72, Fregosi's average shrank to .232 with only five home runs. He opened the 1973 campaign on the Mets bench and in June was peddled to the Texas Rangers.

In translation, then, the Angels acquired Nolan Ryan (and three other players) for the waiver price.

So comprehensive was Fregosi's failure as a Met that the Angels would have had the better part of the deal even if Nolan Ryan had not been a part of it. Catcher Estrada failed to make the Angels roster, and pitcher Rose had a decidedly unspectacular half-season in Anaheim, winning only one game. But Leroy Stanton became a fixture in the Angels outfield. He never attained stardom but gave the Angels five seasons, so a Stanton-

for-Fregosi deal could have caused the Mets some embarrassment.

But it was Nolan Ryan's mound achievements that set the seal on baseball's worst trade.

THE METS ostensibly gave up on Ryan in the belief that his "wildness" would never be cured. Wild? Nolan Ryan was never wild, not the way Sandy Koufax was in his youth. There's even some thinking that young left-handers are supposed to be wild, but it's inadmissible in orthodox throwers. The point is that Nolan Ryan as a Mets pitcher was always around the strike zone if he wasn't quite in it. And popular belief persists that the American League strike zone is an inch or so higher than the National's. For Ryan, that could have made the difference.

Something certainly made a difference. Ryan in the National League had a 9-to-7 strikeout-to-walk ratio that immediately became better than 2-to-1 in the American League. In his eight years with the Angels, he led his league in strikeouts seven times, and both major leagues in six of the seven.

And he was a winner. There has always been a hint of detraction — that Ryan for all his extraordinary achievements has been only a .500 pitcher or only slightly better than that. But throughout a career of service to doggedly mediocre teams, he always was matched against the

best fellow the other club could throw. Ironically, Ryan will be most vividly remembered, historically, as a Texas Ranger. But the Angels years illuminated Ryan at his peak. Of his 302 victories entering the 1991 season, 138 were recorded during his eight-year Angels tenure, including 62 in his first three California seasons.

And oh, the New York press howled. The trade they had lobbied for and briefly rejoiced in became, by benefit of hindsight, a folly equivalent to the Red Sox selling off Babe Ruth to the Yankees way back when.

Nolan Ryan never was traded again. In 1980 he signed on with the Houston Astros as a free agent. Nine years there, and then the Astros made a disastrous miscalculation and let him get away, squandering unprecedented promotional opportunity while 5,000 strikeouts and 300 victories were pending. Again a free agent, he became a Texas Ranger for the 1989 season . . . and the rest is vibrant, ongoing history.

Not since his walk-on appearance in the 1969 classic has Nolan Ryan pitched in a World Series, and he certainly would like to. He was a member of National League division champion editions twice, but the '80 and '86 Astros couldn't win the playoffs. Nor could the 1979 Angels, winners in the American League West. That was Ryan's last term as an Angel, and his manager was Jim Fregosi.

ANG
1 9 7

"The marquee read, 'Nolan Ryan versus the Cleveland Indians.' Oscar turned to me and said, 'A good night is 0 for 4 and don't get hit in the head.'"

ALAN ASHBY

CLEVELAND INDIANS

CALIFORNIA STRIKES GOLD IN RYAN

A LAN ASHBY AND OSCAR GAMBLE SHARED A CAB from the Cleveland Indians' hotel to Anaheim Stadium.

"The marquee read, 'Nolan Ryan versus the Cleveland Indians,'" Ashby recalled. "Oscar turned to me and said, 'A good night is 0 for 4 and don't get hit in the head.'"

Ryan, armed with a 100-mph fastball and absolutely no idea where it might be headed, enlivened a dreary decade in the history of the California Angels with feats that belied the team nature of baseball. Ryan's name absolutely belonged on that marquee. In 1972, when Ryan began a wondrous eight-year stay in Anaheim, "The California Angels versus the Cleveland Indians" promised all the excitement of a high school poetry reading. "Nolan Ryan versus the Cleveland Indians" – Nolan Ryan versus the American League – promised the incredible, the unbelievable, the distinct possibility you'd frame your ticket stub to prove you were there.

Ironically, by acquiring Ryan, the Angels alienated their own fan base. After a decade of expansion-induced mediocrity, the Angels swapped their most decorated and most popular player, infielder Jim Fregosi, to the New York Mets

· · · · · · · · · B I L L   S H A I K I N · · · · · · · · ·

for a then-anonymous foursome:

Ryan snuck into town with an already legendary fastball and an almost-as-legendary absence of control. But in his first Anaheim start, he struck out 10 and shut out the Minnesota Twins, 2-0. By his last Anaheim start, he'd transcended even Fregosi in popularity.

And productivity. The numbers dazzle: four no-hitters, seven one-hitters, 13 two-hitters, 19 three-hitters. Ryan struck out 383 in 1973, breaking Sandy Koufax's major-league record by one, and led the American League in strikeouts seven times in his eight seasons with the Angels. He led the league in walks six times, shutouts three times.

More than numbers, though, one remembers the snapshots from a decade of dominance.

The freeze-frame from July 9, 1972: Ryan struck out 16 in a one-hit, 2-0 twilight shutout of the Boston Red Sox. "I thought capital punishment was outlawed," Boston manager Eddie Kasko said afterward. "Sending any batter out to face Nolan Ryan at twilight is the same as capital punishment."

The freeze-frame from July 15, 1973: Ryan struck out 17 in his second no-hitter, 6-0 over the Detroit Tigers. Detroit's Norm Cash, about to become the last out, came to bat swinging a table leg before umpire Ron Luciano vetoed the tribute. "But, Ron," Cash pleaded, "I've got about as much chance with this as I do with a bat."

The freeze-frame from August 20, 1974. With the Angels starved for attention, a team of scientists from Rockwell international developed and deployed an infrared radar device expressly to clock The Ryan Express. The reading: 100.8 mph – in the ninth inning.

RYAN RODE his fastball past the "phenom" label baseball bestows on promising youngsters to his status as a true national phenomenon. Prevailing wisdom held that Ryan would, like a meteor, burn brilliantly and then burn out.

In 1979, Ryan himself said he believed Tom Seaver would outlast him. Seaver retired in 1986.

"It is one of life's depressing facts that the older you get, the fewer you fan," *(Los Angeles) Herald-Examiner* columnist Melvin Durslag wrote of Ryan in 1976. "By the time he reaches 40, he may be throwing knuckleballs, unless he is playing first base."

In this era of pitch counts as an almost religious statistic ("Gee, Bob, he's thrown over 100 pitches, so he must be getting tired."), Ryan's Angels workload evokes awe. Lots of strikeouts and lots of walks mean lots of pitches, and Ryan regularly threw 175 per game. Once, he threw 245.

Ryan would lose 1-0, win 1-0, lose 2-1, pitching eight, nine and 10 innings. He would no more second-guess his grind or gripe about his offense than he would pitch underhand.

"He lost more close games than anybody I've ever known," said Angels coach Jimmie Reese, a veteran of 75 years in professional baseball, who once roomed with Babe Ruth on the Yankees. "We never got him any runs, but he never complained. I never saw a man like that."

Can't much blame a manager for sticking with a tired Ryan over the fresh arms of "closers" like Lloyd Allen, Dave Sells, Orlando Peña and Don Kirkwood. In Ryan's first four years with the Angels, the bullpen saved 16, 19, 12 and 19 games.

"We didn't have much of a bull-pen," said Chicago White Sox Man-ager Jeff Torborg, who caught Ryan's first no-hitter in 1973. "We didn't have much of a team. It was almost like he had to pitch a shutout to win."

IN 1976, in fact, Ryan led the league in shutouts *and* losses. Ryan's record with the Angels – 138-121 – reflects far more his team's deficiencies than his excellence. So it is almost cruel that after the Angels captured their first division champi-onship in 1979, Ryan felt forced to jump ship to the Houston Astros.

Ryan led the league in strikeouts and shutouts that season. He went 16-14, and General Manager Buzzie Bavasi chased Ryan out of town

with the parting shot that the Angels could find two pitchers to go 8-7 apiece. Bavasi has since called that his worst decision.

Ryan did not want to defect, but after the Angels refused his three-year, $1.2-million proposal before the season, he declared free agency and signed with the Houston Astros for three years and $3.5 million. Before Ryan departed South-ern California, he published an open letter wishing the best to his teammates and to Angels owner Gene Autry, who did not interfere with Bavasi and whom Ryan still counts as a close friend.

"But my greatest joy and satis-faction," Ryan wrote, "has come from the Angel fans who have given me their support and enthusiasm and have provided me with additional strength. I shall miss you all very much, but I will never forget you and your cheers and your loyalty."

They never forgot him either. After nine years with the Astros, Ryan returned to the American League by signing with the Texas Rangers. On July 6, 1989, Ryan pitched in Anaheim Stadium for the

first time since leaving the Angels: The marquee read "Nolan Ryan versus the California Angels."

THEY SAVED their ticket stubs that night. Ryan shut out the Angels, striking out 12. Bob Hope appeared in a pre-game ceremony that night. The crowd remained seated to cheer Hope, but stood to serenade Ryan. Hope was a national treasure; Ryan was *their* treasure.

Said Texas Rangers third baseman Steve Buechele, who grew up in the vicinity of Anaheim Stadium: "I don't want to sound like Nolan's really old, but my dad used to take me to the games here when I was a little kid. There wasn't anything more exciting than coming to the games and watching Nolan pitch."

Two banners told the story that evening. One read, "Welcome Back Nolan." The other read, "Nuke Bavasi."

Most Pitchers Don't Stack Up (*it doesn't get any "batter" than this*) . . . . *Nolan became the seventh pitcher in American League history to strike out more than 300 batters in a season, September 25, 1972. Ryan recorded his 302nd strikeout for the year, defeating the Texas Rangers, and treated himself to 302 silver-dollar pancakes served by Dallas chef Isaac Piña.* (UPI/BETTMANN)

	9:50	1 2 3 4 5 6 7 8 9	R	H	E
	ANGELS	2 0 0 0 0 1 0 0 0	3	11	0
	ROYALS	·0 0 0 0 0 0 0 0	0	0	0

BALL 0   STRIKE 0   OUT 2

AT BAT
26

A Sharp Learning Curve.
On June 19, 1973, only four days after his second no-hitter, Nolan almost repeated his new trick, as he held the Orioles hitless through seven innings. Baltimore rallied and defeated California 3-1. This grip creates the elusive curveball. (AP/WIDE WORLD PHOTOS)

The First No-Hitter, May 15, 1973. *Nolan fires the first pitch to the last batter of the first Nolan "no-no." Amos Otis left the plate hungry after belting a shot to the wall. Angels right fielder Ken Berry jumped up and robbed Otis of the hit, and the Angels topped Kansas City 3-0. (Shortstop Sandy Alomar watches the action from one of the best "seats" in the house. Almost 18 years later, Alomar's son Roberto had an even closer view as he became the final out of Nolan's seventh no-hitter.)* (UPI/BETTMANN)

Great MOMENTS

And Two Months Later . . .

Nolan accepts congratulations from Angels manager Bobby Winkles after hurling his second no-hitter, July 15, 1973. Art Kusnyer, right, filling in for an injured Jeff Torborg, caught the 6-0 win over Detroit. Only five pitchers have duplicated no-hitters in one season. From left, below: Johnny Vander Meer, *consecutive* no-hitters, Cincinnati, 1938; Allie Reynolds, New York Yankees, 1951; Virgil Trucks, Detroit, 1952; Jim Maloney, Cincinnati, 1965; and Nolan, Angels, 1973.

(LARGE PHOTO: UPI/BETTMANN. SMALLER PHOTOS: JOHNNY VANDER MEER, ALLIE REYNOLDS, VIRGIL TRUCKS, NOLAN RYAN: AP/WIDE WORLD PHOTOS. JIM MALONEY: THE SPORTING NEWS.)

JOHNNY VANDER MEER, REDS, 1938

ALLIE REYNOLDS, YANKEES, 1951

VIRGIL TRUCKS,
TIGERS, 1952

JIM MALONEY,
REDS, 1965

NOLAN RYAN,
ANGELS, 1973

*After the second no-hitter,
Ruth serves a cold drink to
the hottest pitcher in baseball.
She reminds him to save his
energy for the mound, as
20-month-old Reid enjoys
quality time with his father.*

(UPI/BETTMANN)

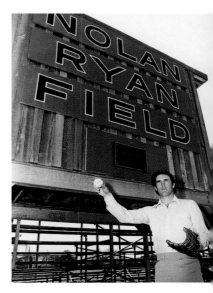

*Alvin High School renamed
its ballpark to honor the
hometown hero after his
second no-hitter.* (COURTESY

RUTH RYAN)

Great
MOMENTS

Angels encircle Nolan as he leaves the mound, a third no-hitter under his wing, September 28, 1974. The Angels rose over the Twins, 4-0. (COURTESY RUTH RYAN)

Nolan displays a game ball from the third no-hitter. In the game's closest play, shortstop Rudy Meoli dived for the ball, made the catch, rose up and threw out the batter to save the no-hitter. Nolan reportedly gave each California player on the field a personal bonus. (COURTESY RUTH RYAN)

California's two hottest stars – one known for motion pictures, the other for pitching motion – choreograph for the camera.

(COURTESY CALIFORNIA ANGELS)

Nolan Invents 'The Wave'? *Nolan's pregame ritual of stretching and conditioning resembles an attempt to encourage fan participation, June 1975.*

(JOHN G. ZIMMERMAN/SPORTS

ILLUSTRATED)

Nolan became the third man in history to strike out 300 batters in consecutive seasons with this pitch to Boston's Carlton Fisk. (AP/WIDE WORLD PHOTOS)

Ryan set the all-time season strikeout record, 383 Ks, breaking the previous mark set in 1965 by Nolan's hero, Sandy Koufax. The Minnesota Twins' Rich Reese became the 383rd victim on September 27, 1973. The Angels won 5-4 in 11 innings. (UPI/BETTMANN)

Broken By The Best.
Home Run King Hank Aaron spoils Nolan's bid for what might have been consecutive no-hitters, June 6, 1975. Aaron's hit kept Johnny Vander Meer's 1938 back-to-back record intact, but the Angels blanked the Brewers 6-0. (UPI/BETTMANN)

Nolan's "right-hand man," Reid, 2, inspects the most powerful arm in baseball, September 1973. Nolan had just struck out 16 Minnesota Twins the previous night, breaking Koufax's record of 383 Ks. (AP/WIDE WORLD PHOTOS)

Bob Feller's American League record of 18 Ks in a single outing fell to Nolan August 12, 1974, as he manhandled the Boston Red Sox. The game also tied the major-league record of 19 recorded by St. Louis Cardinal Steve Carlton in 1969 and the Mets' Tom Seaver in 1971. (UPI/BETTMANN)

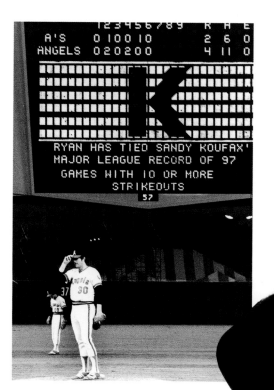

Ryan matches Koufax's "fireworks," tying the record of 97 games with 10 or more strikeouts, Independence Day, 1977.

(AP/WIDE WORLD PHOTOS)

The California ace's body language spells out d-i-s-b-e-l-i-e-f after first base umpire David Phillips rules Nolan has committed a balk, sending Minnesota's Lyman Bostock to the second bag, June 16, 1977.

(AP/WIDE WORLD PHOTOS)

Hospital patients hope to visit Nolan, as the "actor" waits to be examined in "Ryan's Hope." In 1975, ABC featured Nolan's debut. The "soap" portrayed Nolan being injured in a game of basketball. The "television Nolan" had to sneak into the hospital for tests, attempting to keep the team management in the dark. (AP/WIDE WORLD PHOTOS)

Nolan inspects the scientific equipment Rockwell International scientists used to "clock" his fastball at 100.8 and later 100.9 mph. Ryan believes he has pitched faster, and many agree.

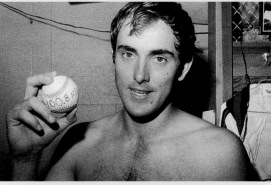

Nolan held up the ball that was timed at 100.8 mph during an Angels game, August 20, 1974 – after it had cooled down.

Coaches and players surround Nolan after his fourth and final California no-hitter, June 1, 1975. Angel catcher Ellie Rodriguez assisted behind the plate in a game that featured Nolan's heat in excess of 90 mph and the extremely deceptive curves and change-ups of a pitcher – not just a thrower. The Angels shut out the Orioles 1-0. (UPI/BETTMANN)

For California, Nolan pitched as many no-hitters as he could hold in the palm of his hand. Flanked by catcher Ellie Rodriguez, left, and Manager Dick Williams, Nolan grips the valuable balls after he no-hit the Baltimore Orioles.

(AP/WIDE WORLD PHOTOS)

**IT** was the absolute worst time for the California Angels to . . . . take a stand against the rising tide of baseball economics. The same team that jumped feetfirst into the free-agent market only a few years before suddenly got cold feet when the greatest pitcher in the club's history became eligible for free agency.

Nolan Ryan had just accompanied the Angels to their first American League West title. He was the most exciting, the most overpowering, the most intimidating pitcher in the game. He commanded millions, and he was worth every cent, but Angels Executive Vice President E.J. "Buzzie" Bavasi apparently let a personality conflict with agent Dick Moss and a personal aversion to the free-agent re-entry process irrevocably alter the future of the franchise.

It was Bavasi who scowled that he could buy "two 8-7 pitchers" to replace Ryan in the Angels' rotation, and those words would come back to haunt him after a couple of later free-agent acquisitions – John D'Aquisto and Bill Travers – proved that quantity is not quality.

There was no one in Angels' history quite like The Express, who would put Anaheim Stadium on no-hit alert every time he took the mound. Sure, there had been Angel no-hitters before. Bo Belinsky pitched one his rookie year. Clyde Wright threw one in 1970. But Ryan was a no-hitter waiting to happen, and the suspense built quickly if he held the opposition hitless in the early innings.

He was, for a time, the only reason to go to the Big A. The Angels organization developed a hard-throwing left-hander to complement him in the rotation, but as exciting as the young Frank Tanana was, it was Ryan who put them in the seats. It was Ryan who kept the '70s from being another decade of despair for the hapless Angels.

It shouldn't have taken a major stretch of the imagination to envision Ryan as a major force in the '80s, but Bavasi convinced himself and owner Gene Autry that it would be foolhardy to give that kind of money to a guy who was pushing 33. How much longer could that arm hold up under the strain of Ryan's 98-mph fastball? How much longer, indeed.

Two years later, the Angels would come up one victory short of the World Series. They have come up a game or two short on several occasions since. How much of a difference Ryan might have made is anyone's guess, but Autry is convinced that it would have been significant.

"I should have gotten more personally involved in that situation," he said several years later. "If I had, I don't think Nolan would have ever left."

The Angels felt the loss almost immediately. Ryan left a giant hole in their starting rotation, and a series of pitching injuries in 1980 kept the club from filling it. He went on to Houston to average 14 victories per season in the '80s, and leave room to wonder if his presence might have saved the Angels the trouble of trying to reinvent themselves year after pennantless year.

HOW COULD THEY let him get away? It was unthinkable at the time, and it is incredible to this day. Ryan wasn't just a Hall of Famer in the making. He wasn't just a strikeout machine. He certainly wasn't just a .500 pitcher, as his detractors maintained, when he was compared to other pitching greats of that time. He was a model player, a great family man, a pillar of the community, all of which was somehow lost in the unfriendly negotiations between Bavasi and Moss.

Bavasi would later admit that allowing Ryan to sign with the Houston Astros was one of the biggest mistakes of his front-office career. Autry has mourned Ryan's departure for years and even tried to bring him back for the 1989 season. The Angels, who in 1979 succumbed to the conventional wisdom that pitchers are ready for pasture in their middle 30s, tried to give Ryan $1.5 million to pitch in his 42nd year. It was an organizational admission of guilt that came 10 years too late to make any real difference, but no one realized at the time that conventional wisdom and Nolan Ryan had long since parted company.

Perhaps the Angels got a little full of themselves. The 1979 AL West title was won largely at the plate, running afoul of the popular notion – still popular, in fact – that it is pitching that wins championships. The club averaged more than five runs per game and had to carry the pitching staff on occasion. The team motto was "Yes We Can," and they did, so who was to say that they couldn't keep doing it without the guy who was asking for the world?

The signs of decline seemed unmistakable. Ryan was 26-27 in his final two seasons in California. He had been on the disabled list for three weeks in 1978 and had left a game in August of 1979 after feeling something pop in his elbow. His strikeout numbers had dropped significantly two years running, though he routinely led the American League in that department. Ryan had averaged more than 300 strikeouts a season from 1972 to 1977, but he had just 223 in 1979. The diminishing K-ration also reflected a decline in innings pitched, but that was partly the result of an industrywide move from four-man to five-man starting rotations.

No one could have known that Ryan would still be pitching 12 years later. No one would have imagined that he would strike out 301 batters at the age of 42. No one had reason to believe he had nearly 150 victories left in that amazing arm. But even in 1979, it was obvious that he had a lot left to offer.

Longtime manager Gene Mauch, who would come to the Angels not long after Ryan left, never marveled at the accomplishments of the truly great players. He would matter-of-factly point out that special people do special things and leave it at that. Ryan was one of those special people, but the California Angels didn't realize it in time.

AST

"I like the National League, and I'd like to pitch there again sometime before my career is over. I'd really like to finish up with Houston if I had a chance."

NOLAN RYAN, JULY 28, 1973

Houston Astros
1979-1988
106 Wins
94 Losses

Astros all-time
strikeout
leader (1,866)

1981
• September 26:
  Threw fifth
  career
  no-hitter
• Astros MVP
• Compiled
  league's lowest
  ERA (1.69)
• Allowed only
  two homers in
  149 innings
• Threw a two-
  hitter to defeat
  Los Angeles in
  Game One of
  the Western
  Divisional
  Championship
  Series

1982
• Won 16 games
• Third in
  National
  League
  strikeouts (245)

1983
• Broke Walter
  Johnson's
  major-league
  strikeout record
  of 3,508

1984
• Third in
  National
  League
  strikeouts (197)

1985
• Third in
  National
  League
  strikeouts (209)
• Captured 100th
  National
  League victory

1986
• Sixth in
  National
  League
  strikeouts (194)
  despite injuries

1987
• First player in
  history who
  was not
  awarded the
  Cy Young
  Award after
  leading the
  league in
  strikeouts (270)
  and ERA (2.76)

1988
• Allowed only
  four runs in
  final 41 innings
  before his
  season ended
  on September
  19 due to
  hamstring
  injury
• Led the
  National
  League with
  228 strikeouts

RETURN OF THE PRODIGIOUS SON

SOMETIMES DREAMS COME TRUE. This marriage of the shy, good ol' country boy from Alvin and the major-league team 26 miles up the road in Houston was strictly storybook stuff.

"Pinch us," said the Astros' faithful; "We're dreaming." Here were the Astros, who built and lost a 10-game Western Division lead in 1979, yearning for one final piece to their championship puzzle as the 1980s dawned.

And who else was better qualified to help take the long-suffering Astros over the top than the man with the mother of all fastballs? John McMullen didn't know an RBI from a UFO when he bought the Astros in 1979, but he knew enough to know he wanted Nolan Ryan.

At any price.

Even though it was speculated that Ryan probably would have signed for less, McMullen willingly anointed Ryan with $4.5 million over four years—about half of what the team grossed in 1979—making him the richest baseball player in history.

Not only was Ryan a future Hall-of-Famer, but he also saw baseball's financial future more clearly than anyone. "Won't be too many more years before this kind of money ($1 million per year) is commonplace," Ryan said. Was he a prophet or what?

McMullen acknowledged his eagerness to outbid Milwaukee and Texas, which also had free-agent interest. "We may end up spending too much, but no one

· · · · · · · · · · **K E N N Y   H A N D** · · · · · · · · ·

PRECEDING PAGES: RONALD C. MODRA/SPORTS ILLUSTRATED

can blame us if it's Nolan Ryan," McMullen told Nolan's agent, Dick Moss.

If only McMullen had felt the same way near the end of the decade.

But nothing – repeat, nothing – could sully Ryan's accomplishments in nine years as an Astro. The fifth no-hitter in 1981; the 1,866 strikeouts; the 1,855 ⅓ innings; the  thrill of the 106 victories and the agony of the 94 defeats. Each of his 282 starts was a thing of beauty. Ryan truly became one of the wonders of the world with each 98-mph heater.

The Houston Era began when the California Angels failed to appreciate his prowess and allowed him to become a free agent after '79, then-General Manager Buzzie Bavasi uttering those famous words: "We'll just go get a couple of 8-7 pitchers."

But two starving artists don't replace a Rembrandt, Buz, and the picture Ryan painted in Houston was a masterpiece. The only thing that upset McMullen initially was that *The Houston Post* broke the story of the signing prior to the announcement. "We had to discard our plans of having Nolan jump out of a cake, *à la* Marilyn Monroe," said McMullen.

OH, SURE. Nolie would have jumped out of a cake . . . when a cow jumps over the Astrodome. Two things haven't changed about Nolan,

his velocity and his low-key personality. He was proud to be an Astro and the Astros were proud to fit him for a rainbow-colored uniform.

From 1980, when he pitched them to within six outs of the World Series, through 1988, when McMullen misread Ryan's free-agent market value and let him go for nothing, Ryan gave Houston baseball nuts a special rush with every one of his trademark windups.

"Getting Nolan makes Houston number one for the pennant and World Series," said Hall-of-Famer Bob Feller. "The amazing thing is he hasn't lost his fastball this late in his career. He's past 30 and he's still got it."

Who could have known or predicted, then, that Ryan would be fortysomething and still have it?

But one thing the Astros did know, even at the time, was that they had something special in Nolan Ryan.

"I know of no one else who has ever worked as hard, as long as Nolan Ryan has in camp and over the winter," said Gene Coleman, the Astros' conditioning and strength coach, after assessing Nolie when he arrived for his first spring training. "The man is professional in the purest sense of the word. You can't measure his value to this team."

"He's a class guy," said relief pitcher Joe Sambito.

"Nolan is a fine person, one I admire and respect," said knuckle-baller Joe Niekro.

"A pleasure to associate with," said spot-starter Vern Ruhle.

One Friday night in Cocoa Beach, Florida, Ryan reflected on the potential hurdles, however.

"I'd be kidding myself to say there won't be any jealousy," he said. "Somebody won't like me because of my contract. But personally I'm not going to be affected by any of that. I don't have a big ego, so I don't care what anyone says. I don't need the publicity.

"All I want is to do a consistent job and see the team win the division and then go from there. I'm a big believer in the team, that teammates shouldn't be competing against each other. I have no reason to feel any differently. I certainly haven't detected any hard feelings. I'm sure a lot of people are watching me."

RYAN NEVER LIKED spring training because of the time – generally a month – to work his arm into prime-time shape.

"Because I'm a power pitcher, I don't reach the maximum until my legs can handle the workload, and when you don't rotate your hips for four to five months, it takes awhile to regain the stamina. I used to fret about making the team in spring training. I mean, two to three weeks into spring training, I'd think I'd lost my arm, that I'd never be any good again."

He never liked spring training. But he did it anyway, performing and conditioning with more intensity each year.

Ryan went 11-10 and posted a 3.35 earned run average that first year with the Astros despite a season-long struggle with tendinitis in both knees, plus a month-long battle with back stiffness and soreness. But he gave them 234 innings and 35 starts.

"Nolan Ryan," said Niekro, "has a helluva lot of guts. He's been in a lot of pain, more than he'll ever let on. But that's the kind of guy Nolan is."

One tough Texan. That was Nolan with the Astros. That was Nolan period. He surely wasn't afraid to pitch inside. Most hitters understood that intimidation is part of the game. But one night in August of 1980 Dave Winfield of the San Diego Padres became incensed after dodging two high, inside fastballs in a three-pitch sequence.

Winfield charged the mound, clocking Ryan on the back of the head and on his back. "Hey, he throws too hard to come in that close that consistently," Winfield protested.

T H A T Y E A R Ryan wasn't the only hard thrower. Four other Astros (J.R. Richard, Ken Forsch, Joaquin Andujar and Joe Sambito) threw faster than 90 mph, and then

there was Niekro's knuckler. "You got Ryan one night, Niekro the next night and J.R. the next night," said backup catcher Luis Pujols. "Make a catcher sweat and get no sleep!" Not to mention the problems this created for the opposing hitters.

By 1985, Ryan had become the first pitcher in major-league history to surpass 4,000 strikeouts. Danny Heep of the Mets, an ex-Astro who had been traded for Mike Scott, was the victim on July 11 in the Astrodome.

That same year Ryan joined an elite fraternity of pitchers that has won more than 100 games in each league. The list included the good company of Cy Young, Jim Bunning, Gaylord Perry and Ferguson Jenkins.

The following season, 1986, he wrestled with a sore right elbow and twice was placed on the disabled list with a sprained medial collateral ligament. Yet he came back to pitch effectively under a 100-pitch limitation. The Astros again won the division and Ryan, 12-8, was one of the game's most dominant pitchers during the final four months.

As was the case in 1980, when the Astros lost that thrilling best-of-five series with the Philadelphia Phillies in the 10th inning of Game 5, the classic '86 best-of-seven playoffs with the New York Mets ended in extra innings – the 16th inning of Game 6.

"It was difficult to take in 1980, and it's difficult to take now," Ryan said.

But some players never are fortunate enough to have felt the joy of a playoff, much less a World Series.

And other players in the past who threw hard never approached Nolan Ryan's longevity. Ryan clearly learned from his Houston experience.

"Everybody goes through transition in baseball," he said. "First you worry about staying in the big leagues. I was one who had control problems, and I didn't know how effective I'd be. But I went from being a thrower to being a pitcher. That gave me some peace of mind.

"I guess I got the feeling that I could make a career, I mean something like a 10-year career out of baseball, after my arm surgery in '75. But I couldn't breathe easy until then. You never can when you're playing on losing clubs. Because every time you go out there, there's a mark on the plus or minus side [wins and losses] and a lot of it is out of your control. But you either win or lose, and all that most people judge you on is your record."

And as for the misinformed who once judged him harshly, saying he was nothing more than a .500 pitcher?

"I'm the style of pitcher [strikeouts] who gets that kind of [negative] attention," he said. "There seem to be a lot of anti-Nolan Ryan people in baseball judging won-lost records, but that's the way it is and you can't change the way people are going to think."

In Houston, they'll always think of Nolan Ryan as a legend. And a state treasure. And a trusted friend.

The Fifth No-Hitter. *Fellow Astros boost Nolan overhead after his unprecedented fifth no-hitter, September 26, 1981, at Houston against the Los Angeles Dodgers. Nolan's 5-0 win included 11 strikeouts, the 135th time in his career he blanked 10 or more batters in a game.* (COURTESY HOUSTON ASTROS)

The Day After. . .
Nolan takes a moment for groundskeeping with Wendy. In contrast to Houston's AstroTurf, the Alvin "infield" grows at a record pace – in 1979 Alvin received 43 inches of rain in a two-day stand.
(AP/WIDE WORLD PHOTOS)

Nolan checks his bunt as a high pitch is fired by a San Francisco Giant pitcher. Houston's Craig Reynolds stole second base on the pitch. (AP/WIDE WORLD PHOTOS)

Ironically, Nolan captures the major-league record of 3,573 strikeouts, July 8, 1983, against the Mets – his first major-league club. Nolan retired 12 batters in the game. Philadelphia Phillies' pitcher Steve Carlton was a close second with 3,569 strikeouts at this point. (AP/WIDE WORLD PHOTOS)

The "Seldom of Swat." *Nolan hadn't seen home plate from a batter's perspective since the 1972 advent of the designated hitter. The Dodger infield had moved in just out of range of Nolan's shoestrings in anticipation on April 12, 1980. Houston Manager Bill Virdon took the bunt sign down and Nolan belted a homer over the left-center-field fence. Nolan tallied six hits that season. His career includes two homers.* (UPI/BETTMANN)

Safe! As the dust settles, LA Dodgers' Mike Marshall scores. But the Astros rallied to defeat the Dodgers 6-4 in this 1985 game. (AP WIDE WORLD PHOTOS)

A little rain can't burst Nolan's bubble. Here he blows a baseball-size bubble as rain covers the field at Shea Stadium. Nolan popped the bubble, struck out the New York Met's George Foster at the beginning of the fourth inning and proceeded to retire the side. (AP/WIDE WORLD PHOTOS)

93

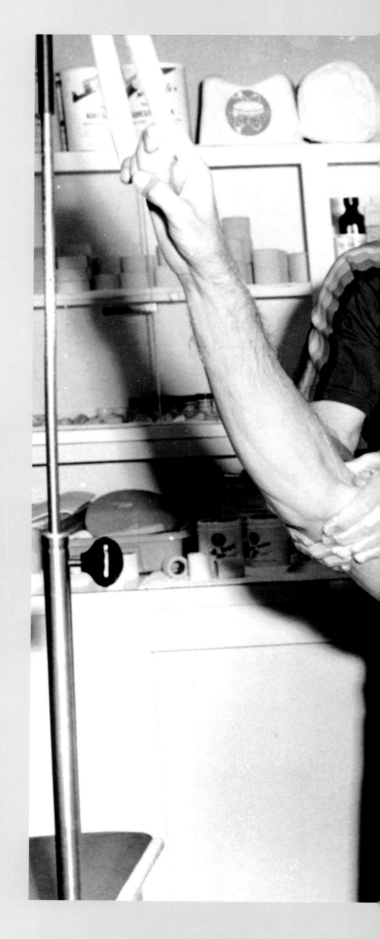

Cleveland Indian legend Bob Feller, left, and Nolan compare fastball grips at the Gillette Hall of Fame exhibit in Houston in 1980. The exhibit traveled to 40 cities to raise funds for the U.S. Olympic Committee and the Baseball Hall of Fame building fund. (AP/WIDE WORLD PHOTOS)

In the early '80s, Morganna became somewhat of a cult phenomenon for three reasons – one of which was her penchant for dashing on the field and hugging sports celebrities. Showing his true sense of humor, Nolan kneels to receive one more award. (UPI/BETTMANN)

Astros trainer Jim "Doc" Ewell, owner John McMullen and catcher Alan Ashby massage the arm that throws the heat that wins the games that packs the house that . . . . (COURTESY HOUSTON ASTROS)

The 4,000th K. *The New York Mets' Danny Heep becomes the 4,000th strikeout victim July 12, 1985. Unfortunately, Nolan didn't tally the win. He was pulled for a pinch hitter with the score tied. However, the Astros recorded a win – after 12 innings.*

(COURTESY RUTH RYAN)

NOLAN RYAN HAS JUST BECOME
THE FIRST PITCHER IN
MAJOR LEAGUE HISTORY TO
STRIKE OUT 4000 BATTERS.

Hats off to the home crowd.
A standing ovation cheers
Nolan after he tallied his
4,000th career strikeout.
Nolan salutes the apprecia-
tive audience. (AP/WIDE
WORLD PHOTOS)

Following page. Arms
negotiations? Nolan is
probably giving then-Vice
President Bush a few
pointers on throwing out
the opening pitch in the
Astrodome, August 28,
1988. Coach Yogi Berra
and Manager Hal Lanier
add to the high-level
meeting. (COURTESY RUTH
RYAN)

Yogi. *In addition to his career as a New York Yankees catcher and his management in Houston, Hall-of-Famer Lawrence Peter "Yogi" Berra is known for his "Berra-isms." When he once said, "It ain't over 'til it's over," was he talking about the longevity of Nolan Ryan?*

(UPI/BETTMANN)

In September 1986, Sports Illustrated featured an in-depth feature on Nolan. SI photographer Ronald C. Modra captures the star in a serious, reflective mood prior to a game.

(RONALD C. MODRA/SPORTS ILLUSTRATED)

The powerful stance and fluid motion of a winning pitcher depend on the legs. Nolan gears much of his training and conditioning to strengthening his legs, in addition to his exercises for the rocket launcher at his right side.

(JERRY WACHTER/SPORTS ILLUSTRATED)

Reese Ryan, top, and Reid, sport the "game face" characteristic of the Ryan family on game day — a look of intense concentration. The two young Ryan men are shown here as batboys in the dugout as the Astros take on the Pittsburgh Pirates, August 1987. (JEFF MERMELSTEIN)

The "boys of summer" become men. Years of battling the elements and opposing batters have given Nolan a distinguished look to match his quintessential Texas charisma.
(CHUCK SOLOMON/SPORTS ILLUSTRATED)

"He provides us with a legacy. For a franchise to have a tradition, it must have legends. Mickey Mantle, Joe DiMaggio and Babe Ruth are legends in New York. Nolan Ryan is a legend in Texas."

GEORGE W. BUSH

TEXAS RANGERS

RYAN SADDLES UP WITH TEXAS RANGERS

T HE TWILIGHT HAD COME to Nolan Ryan's career. But at the age of 42, he was not willing to ride off into the sunset. The competitiveness which had driven him to an excellence and longevity unmatched in baseball history would not allow him to quietly accept what he considered a public slap in the face by Houston owner John McMullen.

Ryan decided to pack his bags one last time.

Nine years after becoming the first $1-million-a-year player in baseball history and being afforded the dream of playing for the Astros, just a short drive from his Alvin, Texas, ranch, Ryan went back into the free-agent world.

Never did Ryan expect his last roundup to turn into what would become the most rewarding segment of his major-league career.

He had bigger financial offers from the California Angels, for whom he pitched in the '70s, and the San Francisco Giants, where Al Rosen, who had signed him with Houston, was the general manager. Ryan, however, decided to accept an offer from the Rangers. At least he would be able to remain in Texas, and at least the travel between his summer employment and Alvin home would be minimal,

T R A C Y   R I N G O L S B Y

making it easier for his family to be part of Ryan's athletic success.

"We talked about it as a family for a long time," said Ryan. "The kids wanted to go to California. They thought it would be real exciting. But Ruth and I looked at the realistic approach. It was the least disruptive, and allowed us the most opportunity to be together as a family."

Signing with the Rangers was all Ryan expected, and more.

"It added to my longevity," said Ryan. "If I had gone somewhere else, I don't think I would have come back after the first year. The players here, the organization's attitude, the fans' support of me and acceptance of me stimulated my desire to play."

THE SUBURBAN atmosphere of Arlington allowed the Ryans to maintain a second home, less than five minutes from the ballpark. The second home also made it easier for Ruth and the kids to spend time at home during the summer when Ryan and the Rangers were on the road – that is, when the family didn't accompany Ryan on the trips.

That made the Rangers more appealing to Ryan, a strong family man. As a strong performer, Ryan's efforts made him appealing to the Rangers and their fans.

The only athlete other than Earl Campbell to be declared an official state hero of Texas, Ryan found an immediate acceptance among the Rangers' fans. He became the hero that the franchise had never been able to create. The question that nobody could answer was whether the Rangers meant more to Ryan, or Ryan meant more to the Rangers.

"He provides us with a legacy," said Managing General Partner George W. Bush. "For a franchise to have a tradition, it must have legends. Mickey Mantle, Joe DiMaggio and Babe Ruth are legends in New York. Nolan Ryan is a legend in Texas."

H IS DAYS with the Rangers may have been few in comparison with the rest of his career, but they were legendary, and the fans' attention was obvious. In the Rangers' first 17 years, they sold out Arlington Stadium 17 times; in the first two Nolan Ryan years, he pitched in front of 15 home sellout crowds.

Small wonder. After 20 years of solid pitching in the majors, Ryan joined Texas just in time to record his 300th win, his 5,000th strikeout, his sixth no-hitter, his seventh no-hitter and, yes, a near-no-hitter a couple of months later.

Nolan's instant star status with Texas was no accident. It was a free-agent *coup d' état*, skillfully executed

by the Rangers' front office.

"A lot of it has to do with timing," said Ryan.

A lot of it has to do with the fact that Ryan not only was in his 40s, at the end of a Hall of Fame career, but that he was still adding to the legend with his pitching exploits. So Ryan was re-signed by the Rangers in 1991 — a $10-million contract with a salary of $4 million for the '92 and '93 seasons and a personal service contract worth $2 million over 10 years.

After an exciting debut in blue pinstripes with the Miracle Mets, a brilliant career with the navy-blue-and-red Angels and a hometown hero stint in Houston's "rainbow" uniform, Ryan reached the pinnacle of his career dressed as a Texas Ranger. And he will wear a Texas Rangers uniform when he goes to the Hall of Fame.

Nolan Ryan, in stark Ranger white, became the first man in baseball history to register 5,000 strike-outs when he got Oakland's Rickey Henderson to swing at and miss a third strike, to the joy of an Arlington Stadium sellout on August 22, 1989.

Again, dressed Ranger white, he became the oldest pitcher in history to win an All-Star game with two shutout innings of work in the 1989 Classic at Anaheim Stadium.

In the gray and blue of the Rangers, he extended his own career no-hitter record with No. 6 – at Oakland on June 11, 1990. The game was teeming with baseball achievements. Nolan became the oldest pitcher – 43 years, four months and 12 days old – to throw a no-hitter. Additionally, in the 5-0 whipping of the World Champion Oakland A's, Ryan established himself as the only pitcher to throw a no-hitter in three consecutive decades.

The eyes of Texas also will remember Nolan in Ranger gray for an exhibition game against his son Reid, an April 2, 1991, family feud. The Texas Rangers played the University of Texas Longhorns with the younger Ryan on the mound for the burnt orange and the ever-youthful Ryan leading the Rangers. College boosters and big-league backers from around the state packed Disch-Falk Field in Austin to see the Rangers defeat the college team 12-5.

For the "Magnificent Seventh," as the next no-hitter became known, Nolan was clad in the white "home" uniform of the Rangers. The evening, May 1, 1991, was Arlington Appreciation Night to boot. Nolan brought out his best stuff for the 33,439 fans who cheered him through a near-perfect game. It was the destiny of the Toronto Blue Jays to join the ranks of Ryan's record book.

Only 10 months earlier, Ryan became the 20th pitcher of all time –

the fourth oldest – to win 300 big-league games when he beat Milwaukee on July 31, 1990.

"MY AGE probably has something to do with the public reaction," said Ryan. "It hasn't been like I was just trying to play one more year, but I'm continuing to perform at a competitive level."

And the impact he has had on the sporting public in his days with the Rangers was brought home to Ryan on a road trip to Kansas City in June 1991.

"Two different men came up to me at Royals Stadium and said their dads brought them to the game in Kansas City when I threw my first no-hitter [for California on May 15, 1973]," said Ryan. "Both of them brought their kids to watch me. They were doing something their dads had done. My longevity has enabled me to go through three generations of fans."

BUT ALONG WITH the longevity of a 44-year-old comes aches, pains and other reminders that the clock is ticking, even for Nolan Ryan. In July 1991, his personal "ticker" became the subject of sports pages across the country. Chest pains put the pitcher on the "ER list" – sending

him on an early-morning visit to the local hospital. The trouble centered in Nolan's chest but was diagnosed as a strained muscle near the sternum. Baseball fans everywhere let out a loud sigh of relief.

But business-as-usual Nolan recovered quickly and raised Ranger fans' blood pressure again, only a few days later in Arlington. On July 7, 1991, Nolan no-hit the Angels through seven innings. California's Dave Winfield broke the spell with a single in the eighth. Nolan tossed down the rosin bag and continued business as usual. In the heat of the game, Nolan established a Rangers' team record, fanning seven batters in a row.

It is that intensity, the heat of Nolan Ryan, that allowed the folks in Arlington and the rest of Texas to embrace a hero of their own, even if it came near the end of Nolan's long career in the fast lane. Even the Texas Senate jumped on the Ryan road trip in March 1991, voting 28-3 to rename Texas State Highway 288. Now known as the "The Nolan Ryan Expressway," the South Texas stretch of road passes nearby Nolan's home in Alvin. The thoroughfare may or may not become one of the most notable "speed traps" in Texas, but its name will always add new meaning to the state's unofficial highway motto, "Don't Mess With Texas."

The 5,000th K. *Strike Three. Determination is written on Nolan's face, ear-to-ear, as he throws the third strike to his 5,000th victim, August 22, 1989.* (COURTESY TEXAS RANGERS)

It had to happen to someone . . . . *Oakland's Rickey Henderson entered the record book as the 5,000th batter to fall prey to the pitching of Nolan Ryan. Henderson appears to be checking for the call – the ball is already in the catcher's hand – but the call is yet to come.* (LOUIS DELUCA/DALLAS TIMES-HERALD)

Strike three.

(AP/WIDE WORLD PHOTOS)

After the game, Commissioner Bart Giamatti brought together two great competitors for this shot featuring the "King of Ks" and the "Prince of Thieves." (Fate brought the pair back together on June 11, 1990, as Henderson became the next-to-last out of Nolan's sixth no-hitter. On May 1, 1991, the two came together in fans' minds: Nolan threw his seventh no-hitter on the same day Henderson earned the stolen-base record with 939 offenses.) Rich Levin, director of public relations for Major League Baseball, backs up Giamatti.

(AP/WIDE WORLD PHOTOS)

The Sixth No-Hitter.

Nolan broke a sweat, but his concentration was infallible, on the mound and in the dugout, during the sixth no-hitter, June 11, 1990. The Rangers crushed the Athletics 5-0 in Oakland.

(AP/WIDE WORLD PHOTOS)

The crowd showed commendable foresight. As Nolan Ryan's early-inning fastballs popped into the glove of catcher John Russell, the murmurs stretched from the field-level seats to the upper deck.

A slice of baseball history was forming on that cool Monday night at the Oakland Coliseum. Inning by inning, strikeout by strikeout. The game between Texas and Oakland turned into a grand stage, the platform for Ryan to move one step deeper into the record books.

On June 11, 1990, for the sixth time in his storied career, Ryan scared a team hitless. And not just any team. He dominated the A's – defending World Series champions, renowned masters of bash – in their own ballpark.

Allegiances change, though, when a no-hitter rises into a baseball fan's mind. By the fifth inning, when Ryan struck out the side, the crowd of 33,436 clearly swung into his corner. Outright cheers greeted seventh-inning strikeouts of Ron Hassey and Felix Jose.

They were not alone. Ryan collected 14 strikeout victims, including pinch hitter Carney Lansford with one out in the eighth. Lansford, typically Oakland's third baseman, had not started because of a strained triceps muscle.

As he quickly discovered, the dugout provided necessary sanctuary. Lansford lasted three pitches. Three swings. Three misses. Adios.

"The last pitch he threw me was 93 miles per hour," Lansford said afterward, shaking his head in amazement. "Moving away . . . in the eighth inning . . . forty-three years old."

Ryan's advanced age had company among startling details in no-hitter No. 6. He had come off the disabled list only five days earlier. His aching lower back forced occasional stretching exercises on the mound during the game.

In the dugout, between innings, he received a friendly assist. Reese Ryan, Nolan's 14-year-old son and a Texas batboy, figured he should help Dad. Rangers Manager Bobby Valentine will always remember the sight.

"The thing I get chills about is his son rubbing his back between the seventh and eighth innings," Valentine said. "Then he patted Nolan on the leg, like he was giving him a little pep talk.

"For all I know, he was saying, 'You've only got two innings left. Don't blow this no-hitter.' "

Not this one. After surviving the eighth inning, Ryan opened the ninth by striking out pinch hitter Ken Phelps. That brought up Rickey Henderson, already an important name in Nolan Ryan lore.

A year earlier, Ryan reached the 5,000-strikeout plateau by whiffing Henderson. Now they battled for a different piece of Cooperstown, dramatically reaching a 2-and-2 count.

Then Ryan threw a curveball. Henderson, a swift baserunner, tapped a slow roller toward shortstop Jeff Huson. Huson charged hard and quickly threw to first to retire Henderson.

Huson's momentum carried him near the pitcher's mound, where he pumped his fist in excitement.

"I saw how excited he was," Ryan said. "I told him, 'Nice play.' " Only Willie Randolph remained. His lazy fly ball settled into right

Base-stealing Rickey Henderson saw his name in lights, while the modest pitcher calmly worked through the ninth inning of a no-hitter. Henderson had previously crossed paths with Nolan and was strikeout number 5,000.

(AP/WIDE WORLD PHOTOS)

fielder Ruben Sierra's glove, securing the no-hitter and inspiring a wild celebration.

Russell, the catcher, reached Ryan first. Their embrace provided an emotional and strange picture. Russell had joined the Rangers only 25 days earlier. Released by the Atlanta Braves in spring training, he spent Opening Day of 1990 coaching high school players near Philadelphia.

He was catching Ryan for the first time. Ever. Suddenly, he also was squatting behind home plate in a historic baseball game.

"It was like I was in a coma," Russell said later. "I had no feeling whatsoever. I was numb.

"I had never seen the look in a guy's eyes that he [Ryan] had in his eyes."

That must have been the no-hit look.

Can you spot the winning pitcher? The Rangers rally around Ryan soon after Oakland's Willie Randolph became the final out.

(AP/WIDE WORLD PHOTOS)

Reporters put Ruth on the spot as her husband nears the 300 mark.

(BEATRICE TERRAZAS/FORT WORTH STAR-TELEGRAM)

As Nolan approached the 300th win, Reese accompanied his dad on the road (and around the bases) to witness the historic event.

(JOHN BIEVER/SPORTS ILLUSTRATED)

116

Joe's Barbecue clientele loses control in Alvin as its hometown hero makes his first attempt at the 300th win, July 25, 1990, against the New York Yankees. (AP/WIDE WORLD PHOTOS)

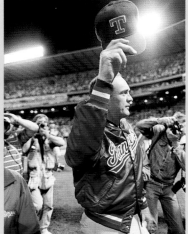

In his second (and successful) attempt at win 300, Nolan and some active Ranger bats defeated the Brewers 11-3 in Milwaukee. Nolan waves his cap to the friendly Milwaukee crowd as most of the 51,533 baseball fans chant, "Nolan, Nolan, Nolan . . . " Baseball scout Red Murff was among the respectful audience. (AP/WIDE WORLD PHOTOS)

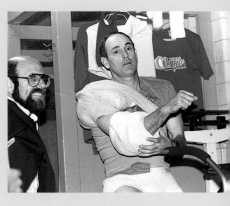

Nolan enjoys a much-deserved "cold one" – an ice pack for his throwing arm, that is – after the 300th victory. (AP/WIDE WORLD PHOTOS)

Home Field Advantage. *President George Bush stops in to visit a fellow Texan and friend before the Rangers' 1990 home opener against the Toronto Blue Jays.* (UPI/BETTMANN)

The Man Of The Year. *Nolan cradles the crystal trophy engraved with "The Sporting News' 1990 Man of The Year" as Editor John Rawlings presents the award in Arlington, Texas. Previous winners of the Man/Woman of the Year, from various sports, include: Denny McLain, 1968; Tom Seaver, 1969; John Wooden, 1970; Lee Trevino, 1971; Charles O. Finley, 1972; O.J. Simpson, 1973; Lou Brock, 1974; Archie Griffin, 1975; Larry O'Brien, 1976; Steve Cauthen, 1977; Ron Guidry, 1978; Willie Stargell, 1979; George Brett, 1980; Wayne Gretzky, 1981; Whitey Herzog, 1982; Bowie Kuhn, 1983; Peter Ueberroth, 1984; Pete Rose, 1985; Larry Bird, 1986; award withheld, 1987; Jackie Joyner-Kersee, 1988; and Joe Montana, 1989.* (D. KENT PINGEL)

Bo knows Nolan – and Nolan knows the brunt of Bo's bat. Bo hammered a grounder that bounced up and caromed off Nolan's lower lip, September 8, 1990. The tough Texan took the shot, threw Jackson out at first, wiped his lip and kept on pitching.

(RON JENKINS/ FORT WORTH

STAR-TELEGRAM)

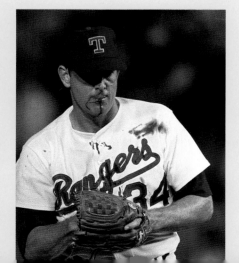

121

Southpaw and former Yale
first baseman President George
Bush throws out the first ball
in Arlington Stadium for 1991, a
year filled with winning streaks
by the Rangers and a perfect win-
loss record for the United States.
(TRUITT ROGERS)

First Lady Barbara Bush enjoys
America's number-one pastime
during the home opener at
Arlington Stadium. (TRUITT ROGERS)

(Right) Nolan Ryan became
an instant superstar with the
Texas Rangers. In his first
season, he led the majors in
strikeouts and had the lowest
ERA for a Texas starter
since 1982. The Rangers
ballclub also selected him as
its "Player of the Year."
(BRAD NEWTON/TEXAS RANGERS)

The Magnificent Seventh.   *May 1, 1991. Nolan Ryan, age 44, retired 27 of 29 batters as the Texas Rangers defeated Toronto, 3-0. Sixteen Blue Jays struck out. Roberto Alomar the final batter, went down swinging. Nolan recorded his 305th career victory and his seventh no-hitter, a record that will not be broken, unless Nolan Ryan throws number eight. The breakdown of pitches . . .*

122   TOTAL PITCHES

83   *Strikes*

39   *Balls*

62   *Fastballs for Strikes*

13   *Curves for strikes*

 8   *Changeups for strikes*

16   TOTAL STRIKEOUTS

 9   *On fastballs swinging*

 3   *On curves looking*

 3   *On curves swinging*

 1   *On changup swinging*

RADAR GUN READINGS

FASTBALL: *High 96 (vs. Carter in fourth), average 93*

CURVE: *High 80, low 77, average 78*

CHANGEUP: *High 86, low 82, average 84*

LAST PITCH: *Fastball, 93 mph.*

After the seventh no-hitter, Nolan described the event as one of his most re-warding achievements because it occurred at home, on Arlington Appreciation Night. Catcher Mike Stanley was the first to congratulate Nolan, who displayed an uncharacteristic burst of excitement after the feat. Stanley made the Rangers team as a non-roster player in the spring. The list of catchers who have shared no-hitters with Nolan is: Jeff Torborg, Angels; Art Kusnyer, Angels; Tom Egan, Angels; Ellie Rodriguez, Angels; Alan Ashby, Astros; John Russell, Rangers; and Stanley, Rangers.

(RON JENKINS/FORT WORTH STAR-TELEGRAM)

(Following page) Nolan is a team player, and when he excels, his teammates join in the celebration. Here, the clenched fists of Nolan Ryan and the Rangers signify that "lightning" has just struck for the seventh time. (RON JENKINS/FORT WORTH STAR-TELEGRAM)

Tour de Jour. *Manager Bobby Valentine, who played center field behind Nolan during the Angels era, chats with his longtime friend after number seven. Ryan, his elbow and shoulder packed in ice, takes his postgame exercise bike tour – just like any other day.* (LINDA KAYE)

At 44, Nolan appeared to be more agile than most men half his age. But it's common knowledge that Nolan stretches and conditions incessantly. In July 1991, a less-than-subtle reminder of his age sent Nolan to the emergency room at Arlington Memorial Hospital at 4 a.m. As news of the incident spread, baseball fans across the country held their breath. The pitcher, experiencing intense chest pains, had feared the worst – a heart attack. "At my age, when you wake up each morning, you start taking inventory," he said later. The pain was caused by a strained muscle near the sternum, an injury Nolan attributed to poor mechanics in his delivery on the previous pitching outing.

(JOHN BIEVER/SPORTS ILLUSTRATED)

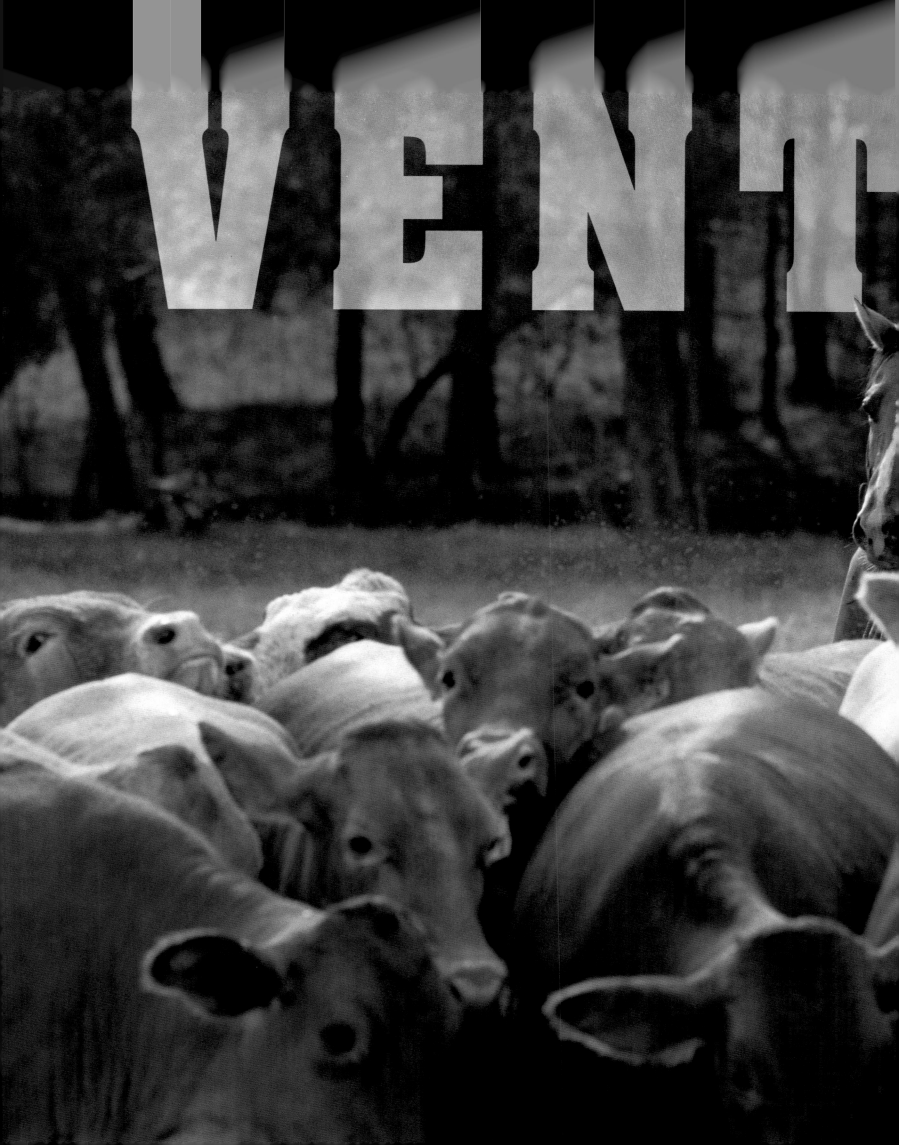

"...It's that very 'real' quality that makes him so genuine and appealing. Forget Kevin Costner and Robert Redford. Think Jimmy Stewart."

BEEF, BANKS & 'SHOW BIZ'

THE EXPERTS WILL TELL YOU that Nolan Ryan's baseball achievements are due to an old-fashioned but reliable recipe calling for equal parts of hard work, self-discipline and natural ability. Off the field, these same ingredients have helped him attain a level of business success that few professional athletes have ever matched. An accomplished rancher, banker and product spokesman, Ryan is unsparing in his support of numerous charitable organizations. He's known as a hands-on manager – whether it's on one of the three ranches he operates in Texas or as chairman of the board of the Express Bank in Danbury. Advertising agencies he works with say that, unlike many of today's superstars, Ryan is unpretentious, easy to talk to and sincerely committed to any product he endorses.

As a businessman, Ryan is adept at determining long-term goals rather than grasping at short-term solutions; before he bought the Danbury bank and changed its name, he spent 10 years on the board of a neighboring bank, learning the ins and outs of the business. That conservative, no-nonsense approach paid off in a big way. Since Ryan took over the reins in 1990, customers eager to be associated with the legendary pitcher have boosted the bank's deposits from $9 million to $14 million. In July 1991, Ryan purchased his former training grounds – the Merchants Bank in Alvin. Combined deposits for the two banks

· · · · · · · **MARCY KORNREICH** · · · · · · ·

are estimated at $34 million. Though most banks are financed by several investors sharing the risk and burden of ownership, Ryan has 100 percent of all outstanding shares of both banks and thus makes 100 percent of the major decisions.

When he's not pitching a ball, promoting a product, running his banks or doing charitable work, Ryan can often be found riding on one of the ranches: China Grove, a 3,000-acre spread in Rosharon; a 2,500-acre operation in the tiny community of Cost; and 3,500 acres in Cotulla, near Laredo, Texas, on which he occasionally runs cows and which he uses as a hunting ranch.

Make no mistake: This isn't a case of some big-name athlete investing big bucks in a business he knows little or nothing about. The man knows his cattle. He rides right alongside the cowhands, helping to pen calves, castrating bulls and dehorn-ing steers, getting involved with the nitty-gritty details of ranching. And, like all of Ryan's investments, the ranches are thriving. China Grove has 550 Braford cows and 30 Beefmaster bulls. (Beefmasters are ½ Brahman, ⅛ Hereford and ⅜ milking Shorthorn.) During calving season, the herd increases to about 1,100. At the ranch in Cost, located

about 157 miles west of Alvin, there are 300 cross-bred cows and 35 Brahman/Hereford bulls; at calving time figure on another 300 four-legged critters.

When he can't be at one of the ranches, he's always accessible to his foremen; no decisions are made without his stamp of approval. He's a good boss to work for, say his em-ployees, because he knows what he's talking about, and he's a good listener. Factor in some shrewd smarts, a little country horse sense and a tight hold on his billfold, and you've got the consummate businessman.

It's been widely reported that Ryan earns $3.3 million a year from the Texas Rangers. That's a bargain. For games when he doesn't pitch, crowds average about 24,000. Each time he's on the mound, more than 32,000 of the faithful flock to see him, boosting revenues from park-ing, tickets and concessions by more than $100,000.

Midway during the 1991 season, Ryan signed a $10-million contract – a salary of $4 million per year for 1992 and 1993 and an additional personal services contract worth $2 million over 10 years after his pitching career.

Ryan's commercial endorsements bring him $1 million to $2 million a year. Add that to his ranching and banking interests, as well as other

investments, and you're liable to come up with a mighty hefty sum. But his business associates say the bottom line about Nolan Ryan – who made only $7,000 his first year in the majors – is that he has never allowed the lure of fame and fortune to rule his life.

Ryan has always been selective about the products he endorses, often sticking with local and regional companies like BizMart® and Whataburger® so he can avoid extensive travel commitments that might take him from his two most important priorities: his family and baseball.

But during the last two years, as he posted even more record-breaking stats, his celebrity status has skyrocketed. Corporate America began to take notice of his prowess in pitching . . . products, that is.

Sports marketing is a huge busi-ness that is growing by 10 to 12 percent a year. In 1989, companies reportedly paid athletes more than $600 million to tout their products. When a company hitches its star to a popular athlete, sales can soar dramatically.

But not just any popular athlete.

To be a truly successful endorser, an athlete must possess that rare combination of visibility, believability and likability, industry experts say. In an era where substance abuse, prima donna attitudes and off-the-field antics are commonplace, Nolan Ryan is an advertiser's dream. He's a clean-cut, bona fide, all-American hero. He's a regular guy, a small-town boy who made it without compromising his values or his morals.

An athlete must be a winner on the field, and his personality must "fit" the product as well as the marketing campaign that is developed. To achieve that perfect fit, advertisers have tailored advertising and promotional programs to best highlight Ryan's perceived strengths. That means his age, his judgment, stability and strong family ties.

When Nolan says he shaves with Bic®, takes Advil® for pain relief, wears Wrangler® jeans and Justin® boots or travels on Southwest Airlines℠, people believe him. He may not be a world-class actor, but it's that very "real" quality that makes him so genuine and appealing. Forget Kevin Costner and Robert Redford. Think Jimmy Stewart.

Ads for both Justin and Wrangler couple Ryan's longevity and his true Western spirit with their products. Justin Boots ads feature Ryan with copy that reads: "Some Things Just Keep Getting Better With Age. Justin Boots Since 1879. Nolan Ryan Since 1947." At Wrangler, Ryan was originally featured in its "Western Originals" series, which featured personalities who embody the concept of the authentic Western lifestyle. Based on the tremendous response to Ryan, Wrangler developed a new series featuring the pitcher and his entire family.

Advil TV ads show Ryan in the locker room, advocating the product for pain relief. And Bic's TV and print ads associate Ryan with its line of dependable disposable shavers.

Ryan's interest and devotion to non-profit organizations is legendary. In addition to fund-raising work he has done for local hospitals, Alvin Community College and Abilene Christian University, he often speaks to local civic and charitable groups.

Sports Sense™, a sports education program, credits Nolan for the program's surpassing its initial projections and reaching high school athletes at more than 13,000 schools nationwide. Sports Sense is co-sponsored by Advil's Forum on Health Education and the National Association for Sport and Physical Education. Nolan and Ruth Ryan have also signed on as spokespersons for Fit Over 40, co-sponsored by Advil and the American College of Sports Medicine. Launched in 1991, the program is designed to help physicians in prescribing fitness programs for the over-40 set.

Over at Justin Boots, Ryan, a rodeo enthusiast, has been instrumental in raising funds for the company's Cowboy Crisis Fund. Established in 1989, the fund provides financial support to severely injured rodeo riders and their families.

EVERYTHING RYAN touches turns to gold, it seems, so it's little wonder that rumors abound about what he'll tackle next. There are plans in the works, observers say, to expand in the banking field. Advertisers keep knocking at his door. Ryan has confirmed that he has been  approached by several different investment groups about buying the Houston Astros.

In 1990, supporters and business associates among the Texas Farm Bureau ranks courted Nolan as a potential Republican candidate for Texas agriculture commissioner. Nolan declined.

"You know, the timing wasn't right," he said. "Later down the road, if that opportunity arises again, I'll just have to consider it. But I don't see myself, per se, going into politics when I get out of baseball. It would just depend on the circumstances."

How To Get Free Airline Tickets, Autographed Baseballs And Dinner With Nolan Ryan.

Dressed for Success.

This popular 1990 Wrangler® poster explains that Nolan is mortal – or at least that he gets dressed in a similar fashion.

(WRANGLER/THE MARTIN AGENCY)

OK, so he's 43 and he pitches no-hitters. He still puts his jeans on one leg at a time.

Cowboy Cut® Jeans & Shirts

Meeting the needs of the "sportsman" – through variety and customer service – was the game plan at Nolan's sporting goods store in Alvin during the early '70s. Five-year-old Aaron Thomas weighs the evidence as he considers a new glove shown by the Ryans. (AP/WIDE WORLD PHOTOS)

NOW PITCHING FOR BIC, NOLAN RYAN.

He wouldn't throw a pitch he didn't believe in.

So when Nolan Ryan says the Bic Metal Shaver keeps him looking good, you can count on it.

He does.

BiC Metal

On The Cutting Edge. *Many celebrities in the macho world of professional sports have endorsed razors and shaving creams. This 1990 Bic® metal shaver ad features the King of Ks and the sharp word play characteristic of Madison Avenue.*

(BIC CORPORATION/SLATER HANFT MARTIN, INC.)

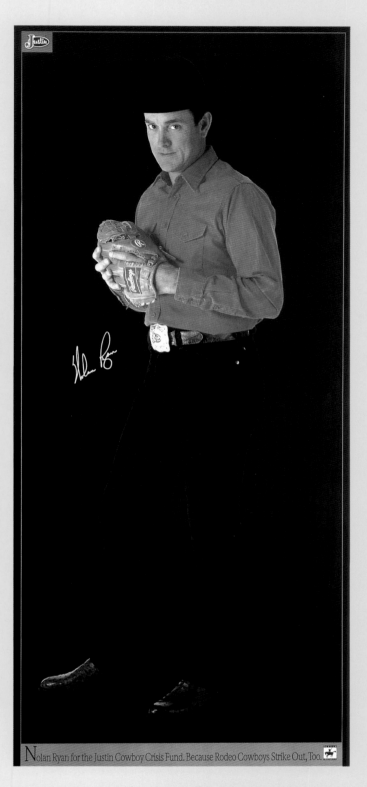

Nolan Ryan for the Justin Cowboy Crisis Fund. Because Rodeo Cowboys Strike Out, Too.

Nolan Ryan helps Justin® support the Cowboy Crisis Fund in advertising and special appearances. This philanthropic group assists professional rodeo competitors and their families in the event of a catastrophic injury or death during Professional Rodeo Cowboy Association/World Professional Rodeo Association-sanctioned rodeos. (JUSTIN/LESLIE HIGGINS ADVERTISING)

Truth in Advertising. *With all of the aches and pains from nearly thirty years of pitching, chances are this "pitch-man" practices what he preaches. In addition to endorsing its Ibuprofen pain reliever, Nolan is a spokesman for the Advil® Forum on Health Education's Sports Sense™ education program, which promotes preventive maintenance to young athletes. The message is: extensive conditioning, proper nutrition and no steroids or performance-enhancing aids!* (ADVIL/DANIEL J. EDELMAN, INC.)

Fortunately for the opposing batters, the headline in this ad is just a play on words from Southwest Airlines.^{SM}

(SOUTHWEST AIRLINES/GSD&M)

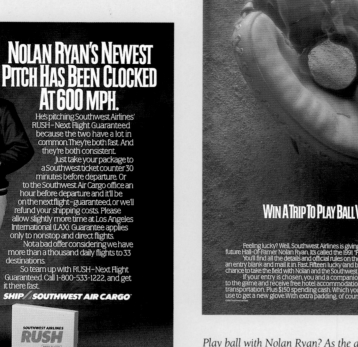

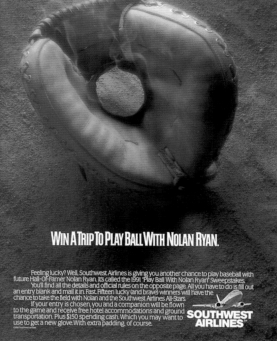

Play ball with Nolan Ryan? As the ad warns, you'd better get a glove with extra padding. (SOUTHWEST AIRLINES/GSD&M)

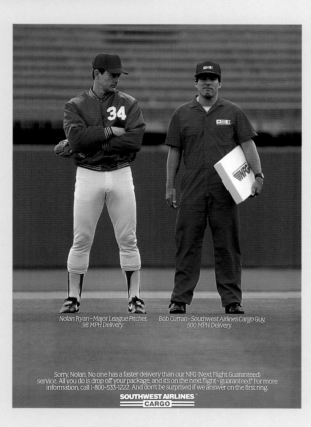

One of Southwest Airlines' 1990 television campaigns featured Nolan in a dramatic series of filmed images – primarily showing Nolan doing what he does best – launching a baseball. Near the end of the "spot" Nolan turns his eyes up to the sky – not to track a fly ball – but to watch other "air traffic" flying over the stadium. (SOUTHWEST AIRLINES/GSD&M)

It may surprise you that there is a man with faster delivery than Nolan Ryan; however, Major League Baseball does not accept Bob Curran's method. (SOUTHWEST AIRLINES/GSD&M)

"Pitching coach"/cinematographer Mick McCormick and Nolan discuss the mechanics required for smooth delivery as they create a "pitch" for BizMart® Office Products Supercenters. (BIZMART OFFICE PRODUCTS SUPERCENTERS/THE SUMMIT GROUP)

"The Heat." *Nolan's heat leaves its mark on a calf as Larry McKim keeps the branding irons ready for the calves on deck.* (RONALD C. MODRA/ SPORTS ILLUSTRATED)

Nolan on the Mount. *Ryan, McKim and company face a Beefmaster on the China Grove spread near Rosharon, Texas.* (RONALD C. MODRA/SPORTS ILLUSTRATED)

142

"NTV." *Nolan's television spots for BizMart feature the pitching ace backed by an infield of office products. The campaign introduced the office supplier's expansion into Houston — "home turf" for one of BizMart's competitors.* (BIZMART OFFICE PRODUCTS SUPERCENTERS/THE SUMMIT GROUP)

"There is no flurry of servants when the King of Ks walks in the front door of this home, where the cordless phone bleeps almost incessantly and the Alvin phone number hasn't changed in 20 years."

LIFE OF RYANS: A SMALL-TOWN LEGACY

THEY ARE A FAMILY AS NORMAL as the heat waves rising out of the prairie grass beyond the barn in Alvin.

The only difference between Reese, Reid and Wendy and their friends, who may fill the swimming pool or track chlorinated puddles onto the kitchen floor of the Alvin ranch house just about any summer day, is that their father happens to be famous.

Ruth and Nolan have raised kids who went to public school because it seemed healthier, who eat at McDonald's after class because everyone else does and who prefer television before homework because that's the way kids are.

Wendy – perky, determined and booksmart just like her mom – likes tennis and cheerleading. And sometimes she's a little jealous that her brothers get to spend so much time in the dugout with Dad.

Reese, who many remember as the son who sat next to his father in the dugout during Nolan's sixth no-hitter, rubbing Dad's sore back between innings, likes baseball and goofing around with the video camera.

Reid is attending the University of Texas at Austin, pitching for the Longhorns – once against his dad in an exhibition game – and is interested in

· · · · · J E N N I F E R   B R I G G S · · · · ·

PRECEDING PAGES: DENNIS MURPHY

147

film production. And sometimes he's jealous of Reese and Wendy, who will get to spend more time with their dad than he did – when Dad finally retires.

Nolan and Ruth credit the domestic normalcy to the constant of a home base in a small town like Alvin, where they also grew up, busted curfews, ate at the Dairy Land and played touch football in the St. Augustine grass of the white-fenced and chrome-plated small-town America of 1957.

Alvin still has the aura of a good place for dogs, pickups and pine trees, a place where people still wave on the street and offer pie to imperfect strangers.

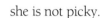
Dating; Christmas, 1966
(COURTESY RUTH RYAN)

O H, T H E R E ' S the occasional cocaine bust during the routine traffic stop, and police scanners

Ruth Holdorff, 1956.
(COURTESY RUTH RYAN)

sometimes reveal the typical banter of the American crimescape of domestic disputes and DWIs. But at least on the surface, Alvin appears untouched by Houston, just 20 minutes to the north.

This is a house in perpetual motion with family life and public demands, but one never too busy if Sue Horner, the retired Alvin tennis

coach's wife, wants to drop off one of her homemade pecan pies Nolan likes so well, Reese and Wendy need a ride to Sunday school or the dog Bea needs a scratch behind the ears.

"The way her and Dad brought us up was, 'You're just like anybody else,'" Reid says. "Just because you have money or you're famous doesn't mean you're better than anyone else."

Reid drives a secondhand Acura that used to be his dad's. He's proud of it. It really is OK if someone leaves a sock on the dining room floor, and it is not uncommon for Ruth or Nolan to come home to a pool full of kids and bird dogs and a hot tub in the throes of an unexpected tsunami.

When Dad attends a graduation ceremony or a football game at the high school stadium, he usually sits in the back row, surrounded by a wife, in-laws and an assortment of other friends and relatives who form an unobtrusive physical roadblock between autograph seekers and the thin, bunched letters that define all Nolan's signatures.

D ESPITE THOSE REQUESTS and the many demands on Mom, Dad and even kids whose teachers send them home with baseballs seeking autographs, it is a home replete with the middle-class normalcy of Ruth and Nolan's own

childhoods of tennis racquets and paper routes.

"My brothers always have people over, and Reid's friends just think it's home," says Wendy, sitting at the breakfast table in their far east Fort Worth summer home.

There is no flurry of servants when the King of Ks walks in the front door of this home, where the cordless phone bleeps almost incessantly and the Alvin phone number hasn't changed in 20 years.

Some ballplayers change them every year.

Usually Nolan goes in the back door anyhow, and the dog Bea is always happy to indulge Nolan – or the guy mowing the lawn – in a little hero worship. Like her owners, she is not picky.

Nolan and Ruth, 1967.
(COURTESY RUTH RYAN)

From Alvin to Arlington, Ruth and Nolan share most of the finances. A secretary helps handle the ranch accounts, working a few days a week at their office in an Alvin bank.

And you're likely to get a busy signal if you call the Ryan house. They answer all their own calls, and he doesn't think it's very nice to tell somebody to wait a minute so you can talk to someone else.

"We've never felt like we had to keep up with the Joneses," Nolan says. "We want our home to be a home where people can feel welcome."

Other people might help with the yard or the pool. Yolanda, the housekeeper, comes in to help wash the dozens of socks, shorts and T-shirts that can be soiled by three teen-agers in a single summer week.

There is outside help here and there, but the Ryans handle their affairs mostly by themselves, just like everyone else.

And like most everyone else, Ruth has concerns about dogs on couches, stains on carpet and junk drawers where rubber bands, hair brushes, screwdrivers, long-expired hamburger coupons and doll parts wait for someone to decide they are no longer needed.

THEY DON'T CALL caterers. The night Nolan threw his 5,000th strikeout, they had a house full of friends and family, and Ruth cooked ham and corn on the cob with rolls for everyone.

Nolan and Reid, 1971.
(COURTESY RUTH RYAN)

Like most anyone, the family shops the grocery stores of Arlington in the summer, making sure there's at least enough whole-grain bread and turkey ham around the kitchen of the leased house to feed the daily onslaught of boys.

Back at their Alvin acreage, the accumulations of family life are more evident.

It is a home as comfortable as its owners – dirty sock here, silk flower arrangement there, working horse saddle in the kitchen, magnetic Rangers schedule on the refrigerator door.

The decor is tasteful but not extravagant.

The kids live upstairs where the bedrooms open into a single living area littered with posters of Michael Jordan and Kareem and even Dad.

There is a classic jukebox in the family room; in the front room is a piano, an anniversary gift from Nolan.

The only indication anyone out of the ordinary is the owner is the trophy case in the family room full of plaques and baseballs, one from win No. 200.

Take away the trophy case and the golden arm, and Nolan Ryan is a regular guy who goes to the Methodist church when he can, got sad when he had to put his good dog Betsy to sleep and likes the pecan pies the retired tennis coach's wife Sue makes.

He has three kids who sometimes wonder if people want to be their friend or they want to say they're friends with Nolan Ryan's kids.

"There's a good and a bad side to it," says Reid, 19. "I've got to go all over the country. I've met Presidents Reagan and Bush. So I'm not complaining. But it can be hard, too."

Like a lot of dads, Nolan doesn't want his 14-year-old daughter to get her ears pierced twice like "all the other kids" and jokes with her, saying she'll be 25 when he says it's OK to date – though his first date with Ruth occurred at age 13.

"I'll probably use that one on him," Wendy says, "but not yet."

NOLAN'S A GUY who says he longs to go to the lake in the summer and ski and fish or drive up to the Rockies in Montana with Ruth and the kids and cast lures into blue mountain waters. His family would like that, too.

But over 20 years in a summer business, part of it being a famous guy in a summer business, means some summer stuff can't happen.

The Ryans.
(COURTESY RUTH RYAN)

Wendy says she would like to go to Six Flags with her dad. Her dad would like to go, too. But it's too disruptive, he says.

Just like any daughter. Just like any dad. Just like any family.

A staple on the Ryan spread, the backstop of the practice field awaits the next barrage. (TRUITT ROGERS)

The picturesque surroundings of the Ryan home near Alvin. (TRUITT ROGERS)

RETIRED high school tennis coach Aubrey Horner sits back in the recliner of his living room in Alvin, just across from the 50-yard line of the football stadium and just a fastball's throw from Schroeder Field, where Nolan Ryan threw the first pitches of his Little-League career and where Ruth, at age 12, peered through the lower rungs of the outfield fence to get a look at the tall, skinny pitcher her sister Lynn "kinda liked."

Horner talks about the once-in-a-lifetime kid a coach comes across. The grittiest, most determined athlete he ever coached.

He isn't talking about Nolan Ryan. He is talking about Ruth, Ruth Holdorff, the one who married Nolan Ryan.

"Ruth is a champion wife, a champion mother and a champion to her family," says Horner, recalling the day he kicked Ruth off the tennis team for "goofing off" (though the move lasted all of 20 minutes – just long enough for Ruth to cry and return with her dad, more determined than ever).

"I have never coached another one like Ruth. I never had another kid with her determination."

You have seen her in photographs, at charity banquets, on television, almost always next to one man, her husband, Nolan Ryan.

Maybe you have even shoved past a blonde, blue-eyed lady in a restaurant or hotel lobby as she accidentally blocked your path to Nolan Ryan.

But there is more to Ruth than Nolan Ryan.

Alvin High School's "Most Beautiful" girl and "Most Handsome" boy were married June 26, 1967, in what some back in Alvin still call a storybook wedding.

By 1968, Ruth was 19 and had barely set foot outside of Alvin. Nolan was 6-9 with the New York Mets with a 3.09 earned run average.

In a dirty Queens apartment, the beauty queen who had cut Goodyear store grand-opening ribbons and won the state tennis doubles title as a sophomore was just another housewife who didn't know a good plumber or how to get to Jersey, and Nolan was just another struggling kid with a wild fastball and an unhappy wife.

"After a year and a half, I knew I was going to have to make a choice here," Ruth said. "I was going to be a baseball wife or get a divorce."

Nolan was just as unhappy. By most accounts, including his own, he would have given up the game somewhere back in New York and returned to Alvin to be a veterinarian, if not for Ruth.

It was Ruth who opted to make the sacrifice, and dedicate her life to a man, a marriage and a game.

Today, Nolan and the kids call Ruth the quarterback. Everyone

helps make decisions, but it is Ruth who carries business cards – a gift from her sister – reading "Ruth Ryan, Director of Internal Affairs, Ryan Residence" and who orchestrates the game plan.

It is Ruth who remembers to make flight reservations for road games and scoop up the dog Buster at the vet's. It is Ruth who knows when Nolan's nephew is coming to mow the lawn, when the gas bill needs to be paid and that someone needs to be called to fix the window in the master bedroom.

And it is Ruth who goes out of the way to make sure the kids remain fairly normal, keeping a healthy outlook in the glare of the spotlight.

"When Dad puts on his scary voice, you listen," Reese says. "She's not very scary, but you listen because you have to respect her."

The kids all remember the time Ruth went through the Burger King drive-through with them in a Gremlin mask. Or how about the time she did that flip on the trampoline? Or that Halloween they all dressed up like football players and Ruth was the coach?

Reid remembers when it became apparent Nolan would not be able to coach Little League like many of the other dads. Ruth was confident and happy to accept the task. She had to quit because, by most accounts, the men were intimidated and didn't want her around.

Ruth may know her baseball as well as she knows the sometimes contact sport of being a mom, but it is the daily competition against Southwest Airlines flight schedules, making sure someone mows the lawn and making sure the car-phone bill is paid – which sister Lynn guesses is probably heftier than her monthly mortgage payment – it is that competition where Ruth is most in demand and amazingly adept.

While other spouses of the famous may be soaking up rays on an isolated beach or dining on fresh endive in a raspberry vinaigrette at the spa, Ruth has larger priorities. Their names are Nolan, Reid, Reese, Wendy, Mom, Dad and other family members.

Ruth might like to spend two weeks at a spa – yes, she can afford it – but that would mean two weeks away from the kids. And who would feed the dogs or make the airline reservations?

"I never thought of myself as rich," says Ruth. "With three kids and traveling it takes up all your money.

"I'm really just happy to be able to go to the mall and buy clothes when we want to." To go to the mall and buy clothes. It is a statement that could have come out of your neighbor's mouth, but it did not. It came from the backbone of one of baseball's greatest, in typical, humble fashion.

When the Ryans were invited to the White House last year for a formal affair with the Queen of Denmark, Ruth's mother was hemming her daughter's gown just hours before the flight to Washington was to leave. Just like any mom. Just like any daughter on the run.

Always enough money, but never enough time, in a world where reporters and fans shove past Ruth as if she were a stray chair blocking the path to Nolan. "I think the wife is the hardest role to fulfill," Nolan says. "I think if anyone is to have a successful marriage in baseball it takes someone dedicated to accomplishing that, and their importance is played down so much by the fans and the public, sometimes they probably don't feel like what they do is appreciated.

"There's a lot of responsibility she has to shoulder outside of what the normal mother would."

"The best ever," her tennis coach says without a pause. "Her determination sets her apart from every other athlete, every student, I have ever had."

Sometimes, in the very public shadow of Nolan Ryan, the motherhood and wife trophies are few.

"I know," Ruth says, "that he'd do the same for me."

June 26, 1967, the wedding. "Marrying Ruth was the best thing I've ever done in my life," Nolan vowed.

(COURTESY RUTH RYAN)

This small frame house was the first home of the Ryans – in the backyard of Ruth's parents' house. (TRUITT ROGERS)

The Ryan family is loaded up for a spin in Nolan's Chevy truck, but where are the keys? Nolan and Ruth look as if they suspect Reid is hiding something.

(COURTESY INGRID HOLDORFF)

Ruth and newborn Reid returned from the hospital just in time to celebrate Thanksgiving with the family in 1971. This shot shows four generations of the Holdorff line, standing from left: Larry Holdorff; Nolan; and Ruth's grandfather, "Pop" Holdorff. (COURTESY INGRID HOLDORFF)

See if you can hit it.
Eighteen-month-old Reid takes batting practice with the King of Ks, July 17, 1973. The proud parent had just pitched his second no-hitter for the Angels two days earlier.

(AP/WIDE WORLD PHOTOS)

A California couple enjoys a night out in Anaheim, 1979. (ANAHEIM BULLETIN)

Nolan and Ruth pose for sports photographers as Nolan prepares to go after Sandy Koufax's major-league strikeout record, September 13, 1973. Ruth's excitement level appears to reach the "warning track" as she alternates with a trance, a yell and a smile. Her husband, on the mound in Anaheim, was rapidly approaching Sandy Koufax's K-mark. (AP/WIDE WORLD PHOTOS)

Wendy Ryan and her grandfather, Larry Holdorff, seem to enjoy Father's Day cards even more than baseball cards, June 15, 1980. (COURTESY INGRID HOLDORFF)

Even in the demanding world of baseball, there are times when father and son can spend time together, somehow making it all bearable. (COURTESY RUTH RYAN)

Two grandmothers are greater than one. Martha Lee Ryan and Ingrid Holdorff make plans to spoil their grandsons Reid and Reese. (COURTESY RUTH RYAN)

Lynn Nolan and Martha Lee Ryan. (COURTESY RUTH RYAN)

Meeting m-i-c-K-e-y. *Ruth, Nolan and Reid introduce themselves to the only mouse that matters in Anaheim.* (COURTESY RUTH RYAN)

Reid cracks up as Nolan opens a birthday gag gift — a pecan. Later Nolan unwrapped an elegant nutcracker intended to accompany the shelled treat, January 1976. (COURTESY INGRID HOLDORFF)

Batter Up! *Nolan and children play jump peg as they wait for the Ryan breakfast of choice — pancakes.* (COURTESY INGRID HOLDORFF)

Larry and Ingrid Holdorff,
1991. (MILTON ADAMS/FORT
WORTH STAR-TELEGRAM)

All Aboard! *Alvin fans charter*
this coach to see their hometown
hero in action.
(COURTESY INGRID HOLDHOFF)

The First United
Methodist Church of Alvin.
(TRUITT ROGERS)

China Grove, Nolan's
ranching concern near
Rosharon, Texas. (D. KENT
PINGEL)

Ranch foreman Larry McKim and his cowdog seem to be doing a little product endorsement themselves, posing in front of an old Pepsi® icebox on the ranch. (D. KENT PINGEL)

Just like family. *The Tom Seaver family is treated to the breakfast normally reserved for family – Mr. Holdorff's Swedish pancakes, fresh from the pan.* (COURTESY INGRID HOLDORFF)

Nolan Ryan Field, home of the Alvin Yellowjackets.

(TRUITT ROGERS)

Thomas McReynolds, Larry McKim and former Houston Astro Harry Spilman take a break before "doctoring" cattle at the China Grove ranch. (D. KENT PINGEL)

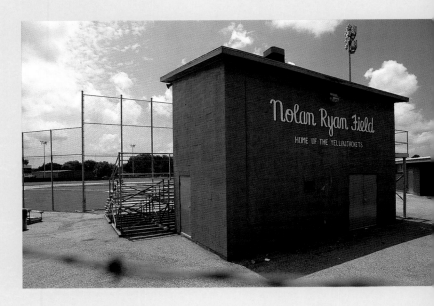

*Ruth and Reid enjoy a
Rangers home game.*
(MILTON ADAMS/FORT WORTH
STAR-TELEGRAM)

They're only posing! *There was no animosity between father and son, despite this impending swing, before the Texas Rangers vs. Texas Longhorns game, April 2, 1991.* (RONALD C. MODRA/SPORTS ILLUSTRATED)

Like Father . . . *In the family tradition, Reid signs an autograph for a young fan in the Longhorn dugout.* (TRUITT ROGERS)

Each pitcher, in typical Ryan style, was complimentary of his opponent's performance after the game. And in typical fashion, they both thought their team should have won. But this time, Dad enjoyed the upper hand, because the Rangers defeated the Longhorns handily.

(AP/WIDE WORLD PHOTOS)

Media representatives from every major city in Texas, the major sports networks and even a television crew from Japan covered the Ryan vs. Ryan game in Austin. (TRUITT ROGERS)

Wendy and a slightly outgoing Reese take the spotlight and the microphone in the postgame press conference after their brother and father went head-to-head on the mound.

(TRUITT ROGERS)

Reid, Reese and Ruth take
time out for Nacho, the cat.

(MILTON ADAMS/FORT WORTH

STAR-TELEGRAM)

Nolan and the women of his life, Wendy and Ruth, 1989.

(JOYCE MARSHALL/FORT WORTH STAR-TELEGRAM)

"I'd get two new pairs of blue jeans for school every September. My mother would wash one pair each night, so I'd always have a clean pair.... In those days we never felt deprived of anything."

NOLAN RYAN, 1981

THE STUFF OF WHICH LEGENDS ARE MADE

THE BOY'S REAL EDUCATION BEGAN under the wavering glare of a corner streetlight in a small Texas town that was like most other Texas towns. There was a barbershop and a picture show, a five-and-dime and a drugstore, a pool hall and a couple of seedy saloons. For the most part, folks went to bed early and got up the same.

Those who did and those who didn't passed through Nolan Ryan's life in Alvin, Texas, in the mid-'50s. His were the inquisitive ears and the wide eyes of a 6-year-old sitting at the intersection of Gordon and Sealy in the middle of the night, watching life unfold before him while he rolled newspapers. Night, after night, after long and dreary night. The boy missed little.

The possums and the skunks, stealing out of the storm sewers to nibble at the popcorn that was swept into the street after the late movie let out. The neon-colored faces that went laughingly into the night when the pool hall and the bars closed. The candy wrappers and paper cups, rattling down the dark and empty street, chased by a lonesome wind.

Just about everything that had to do with Alvin came through that intersection at one time or another. The boy watched and listened and learned.

· · · · · · · · · J I M R E E V E S · · · · · · · · ·

"I saw a lot of folks, some of Alvin's best, down there at night," Ryan remembers. "You name it, it eventually went on down there."

To better understand the man that Nolan Ryan has become, it is essential to get a grasp of the boy that he once was. The values that have helped make Ryan a hero to the American public were forged there in that small Texas town, where he lived and played and worked and grew up to become Alvin's most famous citizen.

Lynn Nolan Ryan Sr.

"I came from a very stable home life," Ryan says. "My parents were home every night. My mother put dinner on the table every night. They were something we could depend on."

LYNN NOLAN RYAN JR. was the youngest of six children born to Lynn and Martha Ryan. Lynn Senior worked for Pan American Petroleum in the daytime and as the Alvin distributor of *The Houston Post* at night.

Nolan – his folks called him by his middle name to distinguish him from his dad – was in the newspaper business from the time he was in the first grade until he graduated from high school.

The wakeup call for Nolan and his brother Robert – seven years his senior – came at 1 a.m. That's when the bundle of 1,500 newspapers landed with a thud on the corner of Gordon and Sealy each morning.

"It wasn't easy getting me up," Ryan admits.

The father and sons would roll papers for an hour, then Lynn Senior and Robert would begin the deliveries while Nolan continued to roll.

"They'd come back for me and the rest of the papers and drop me off at home around 3 or 3:30," Nolan recalls. "Then they'd finish the route. After that, Dad would go on to his daytime job."

And after a couple of hours' sleep, Nolan and Robert would go on to school. Any questions about where Ryan learned his now-famous work ethic?

Nolan did the collecting afternoons after school and on Saturdays, when he'd much rather have been playing basketball or baseball.

"I hated that job," Ryan recalls. "People wouldn't pay you, and you'd have to come back. There was no leash law then, and dogs were always getting after you. It wasn't much fun."

During the summers Nolan added a "real" job to his moonlight work. He mowed lawns. "I had eight or 10 that I maintained every summer," he said. He continued until he was 14, when he got his driver's license. He painted houses one summer and

unloaded boxcars for a lumber yard another summer.

"That," Ryan said, "was the hardest, hottest work I ever did or ever hope to do. It was miserable in those boxcars in the summertime. But if we wanted spending money, we worked."

RYAN GREW UP with an appreciation for the land. An uncle owned a dairy farm at Beeville, Texas, where the family visited on holidays. Ryan, who grew corn and tomatoes and onions in a backyard garden in Alvin, roamed the pastures of the farm, whistling rocks at turtles in the creek, fishing in the pond, exploring the far  corners of the old barn, where dust motes drifted silently in shafts of pure Texas sunlight.

"That's where I decided," Ryan said, "that I had to have a ranch someday."

The man would grow to a mighty destiny, but the boy never forgot the feel of good Texas dirt between his toes. The Ryans lived in a four-bedroom house, two children to each room. They weren't rich, but they weren't poor either. Five of the Ryan children – Nolan being the exception – went on to college.

"We never went hungry," Ryan said. "I can still remember those big Sunday dinners at home after church, with all of us kids there. Mom would cook a big roast or fried chicken, and there would be mashed potatoes and gravy, all kinds of vegetables, like green beans and corn, and homemade biscuits."

"I'd get two new pairs of blue jeans for school every September. My mother would wash one pair each night, so I'd always have a clean pair available. In those days we never felt deprived of anything. Working for what I had taught me the value of things, the value of money."

His parents taught him other values. Lynn Senior, who died of lung cancer at 63, was Ryan's first real role model, a quiet giant of a man at 6 feet 5 inches, 240 pounds.

"He was a person I looked up to," Ryan said. "He was there if I ever needed him, a security blanket. He would come to my athletic events when he could. He never said much, except to be supportive.

"The way he treated my mother, the respect he had for her, was passed on to the kids. That respect is one thing I've tried to instill in my own children. Mothers sacrifice more out of their own lives for their kids than anybody else."

Ryan saw the respect his father gave his mother and the quiet dignity she maintained in running their home. That's how he wanted his marriage, his own home, to be.

That's how it is today with Nolan and Ruth, his childhood sweetheart.

"I'm a believer that when you make a commitment, you make a commitment," Ryan said. "And that's what marriage is. I believe you're only as good as your word. If people can't trust you, what have you got? Where do you establish your values? If you look at our society today, because of the lack of family values, you're seeing more and more social problems.

"When you have kids, you're making a commitment there, too. You have an obligation to give them the best foundation you can give them so that they can go out in the world fully prepared."

NOLAN AND RUTH didn't know quite what they were getting into when Nolan hit the major leagues in 1968. This was a far cry from that street corner in Alvin, Texas. Suddenly the young couple was faced with dilemmas for which they were hardly prepared. Baseball players, like all professional athletes, are fair game for all sorts of temptations. The Ryans learned that not everyone shared the same philosophy about marriage and fidelity.

"We were both somewhat naive about things," Ryan said. "That had never really crossed our minds. You have to decide what's in your best interests and you don't worry about whether it's the popular thing to do. We've all felt peer pressure at times in our lives. You just have to be

responsible for your own actions. Something my dad told me a long time ago has always stuck with me: 'When you tell the truth, you never have to worry about remembering what you said.' "

Asked to describe himself, Ryan started with "conservative."

After that? "Honest. Respectful of other people's rights and feelings. I have a sense of humor that most people aren't aware of," Nolan added. "I've found it interesting that a lot of people have a very different opinion of me before they get to know me, compared to after. People seem to think I'm standoffish, boring, hard to get to know. The exposure I've gotten in the last couple of years has probably given people more insight to me.

"I still represent small-town Texas, and that's fine with me. I'm still like the people who lived where I grew up. I've kept my roots. I'm proud of that. I'm proud to be a Texan."

The boy who once sat on a street corner on a thousand starry Texas nights, listening to the scream of cicadas, the song of the crickets, the whirring wings of the nighthawks, is now the man who hears the cheers, the accolades, the adulation of an entire country.

Strangely, wonderfully, he hasn't changed that much.

173

Working cattle in the heat and humidity of South Texas' climate makes for a sweaty day, even under the shade of a "gimme cap." (COURTESY INGRID HOLDHOFF)

The rancher is equally
adept on the range –
feeding grain to one of his
Beefmaster bulls in order to
build a happy and healthy
herd. (AP/WIDE WORLD PHOTOS)

The Ryans appear at ease
in conversation with
President Richard Nixon
and first lady Pat Nixon in
San Clemente, California.
(COURTESY RUTH RYAN)

Alvin fans turn out in full
force for autographs from
their hometown heroes,
Nolan and Ruth Ryan of
the Miracle Mets, during
Nolan Ryan Day. (COURTESY

RUTH RYAN)

Nolan's unselfish reputation
for marathon autograph
sessions began early and
continued throughout his
career. (COURTESY RUTH RYAN)

Nolan, the picture of youth,
citizenship and ability.

(COURTESY RUTH RYAN)

He got by with a little help from man's best friends . . . . In August of 1974, the California Angels' bats had "gone to the dogs," and Nolan was consoled by Betsy and Gypsy accordingly. This shot was taken the day after Nolan fanned 19 batters and gave up only four hits in an 11-inning, 1-0 loss. Nolan's previous four losses were 2-1, 3-2, 2-1 and 9-1. (AP/WIDE WORLD PHOTOS)

The Ryans gather for a family reunion: seated, Mr. and Mrs. Lynn Nolan Ryan Sr. Standing from left: Judy, Bob, Nolan, Lynda, Jean and Mary Lou.

(COURTESY RUTH RYAN)

Nolan "checks the signals" given by a production person during the filming of his cameo appearance in the "soap" Ryan's Hope.

(UPI/BETTMANN)

Brains & Brawn.

One of the most esteemed students of Alvin Community College participates in commencement exercises, May 21, 1987. (COURTESY RUTH RYAN)

A friendship that began during Nolan's Houston era flourished over the years, allowing Nolan to visit and travel with President George Bush on various occasions. (COURTESY RUTH RYAN)

Nolan hunting with Lionel Garza on the Cameron Ranch in McMaulin County. (COURTESY RUTH RYAN)

The dapper side of Nolan Ryan is evident in this shot, which seems to illustrate that fine pitching is a black-tie affair. (RONALD C. MODRA/SPORTS ILLUSTRATED)

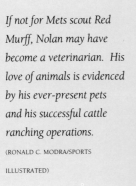

If not for Mets scout Red Murff, Nolan may have become a veterinarian. His love of animals is evidenced by his ever-present pets and his successful cattle ranching operations.

(RONALD C. MODRA/SPORTS ILLUSTRATED)

*Deep in thought, Nolan watches action
in the 1991 exhibition game between the
Rangers and the University of Texas
Longhorns. The game pitted Big Tex
against young Reid, a UT freshman.
The father-and-son shootout provided a
wonderful opportunity for Reid, but also
had the potential for too much pressure
for a young pitcher, according to the
fatherly Ryan.* (TRUITT ROGERS)

"The afternoon knows what the morning never suspected." — *Swedish proverb* (RONALD C. MODRA/SPORTS ILLUSTRATED)

NOLAN RYAN
by BOB PACK

THE DAY EAST MET WEST

Mark Schramm, National Public Radio

"My heroes have always been cowboys..." Willie Nelson

As a boy growing up in Washington, D.C., the West was to me a vast and wondrous place of wind-swept prairies, wild horses and mountains that reached to the sky. In my mind's eye, it was a land of awesome beauty and power, a land of heroes. My heroes were cowboys. Men of strength, skill and courage. Men who sparked the imagination and made little boys dream of other times and places. Men who could turn parked cars and pavement into covered wagons and dusty trails. I never met a real cowboy. But I heard one, once, many years ago. It was in Baltimore's Memorial Stadium on a brilliant summer afternoon. My dad walked me around the ballpark. The ushers hadn't made it out to the right-field bleachers yet, so we wandered to the visitors' bullpen beyond the outfield fence. "Crack!" went the sound of a bullwhip, cutting the air like a thunderbolt. It snapped its way around the park, and just as the echo was almost gone, "Crack!" it went again. I knew the sound. I had tried to make it that very morning on the street in front of our apartment, as I pretended to herd a thousand head of black Angus onto my ranch, snapping my wrist to make the whip hiss like an angry snake. But this bullwhip had a vengeance to it that my whip – a jump rope with plastic handles – could not muster. The cowboy wielding this mighty serpent didn't wear spurs. Nolan Ryan, young, long and lean, kicked dirt out of his spikes, adjusted his cap, gave a laconic nod to the catcher, pumped his leg and . . . "Crack!" The ball exploded into the catcher's mitt, leaving a white spray of rosin in its wake. I pressed my nose close to the fence, too awestruck to speak. My dad, who would put me to sleep at night with stories of Walter Johnson, Smokey Joe Wood, Bob Feller and other great pitchers, told me of Ryan. "He's from Texas. They say he may be the fastest yet," he said. " 'Course," he chuckled, "they say he doesn't always know where it's going." Those were the days when strikeouts, wild pitches and walks occurred with equal regularity for Ryan, whose gifts were so prodigious that the mastering of them would take years. Such subtleties were lost on this 11-year-old; the sound of that bullwhip kept ringing in my ears long after we made our way to our seats. The Orioles were no match for Ryan this day. The catcher's mitt continued to crack through 11 strikeouts in a complete-game, shutout win. After the last out, he didn't ride off into the sunset; he simply walked off the  mound, his head down, and put his bullwhip into his warm-up jacket. The cowboy's day was done.

A DESIGNATED DEITY

Ron Fimrite, Senior Writer, Sports Illustrated

IN ALL OF SPORT, few figures rise to the mythic stature of the fastball pitcher. He is, like Zeus, a hurler of thunderbolts. He is the flamethrower, the fireballer. He brings heat and smoke. And from his flaming fingertips, legends spring forth. Consider Walter Johnson, whose high, hard one led rival outfielder Ping Bodie to complain, "You can't hit what you can't see." Or Lefty Grove, of whom newspaper columnist Bugs Baer wrote, "He could throw a lamb chop past a wolf." The fastball pitcher is a magician who can make baseballs disappear. When his manager asked Jigger Statz where the Dazzy Vance pitch was that struck him out, the Cubs outfielder responded, "Well, I couldn't see it, but it sounded low." Said opposing pitcher Wes Ferrell of Grove: "He'd throw the ball in there, and you'd wonder where it went to." "On a cloudy day," said St. Louis Browns third baseman Jimmy Austin of Johnson, "You couldn't see the ball half the time." Satchell Paige threw the ball so hard in his younger days, said fellow Hall-of-Famer Cool Papa Bell, that "the ball'd be by you so fast you could hardly turn to look at it." Even the nicknames connote speed: Walter "Big Train" Johnson, "Smoky Joe" Wood, "Rapid Robert" Feller, Ewell "The Whip" Blackwell, "Sudden Sam" McDowell, Dwight "Dr. K" Gooden, Roger "The Rocket" Clemens. You could go so far as to say that, except for Bob Gibson and Sandy Koufax, hardly anyone in this fast company has an ordinary name. Instead, you have a Dazzy (Vance), a Dizzy (Dean), two Rubes (Waddell and Marquard) and even a Van Lingle Mungo. And at the head of this swift pack, we have "The Ryan Express," Lynn Nolan Ryan – the speediest of the speedy, the ultimate strikeout artist. Ryan not only has thrown harder than anyone in baseball history, he has thrown harder longer. In 1990, he led the major leagues in strikeouts for the eleventh time, at age 43. He also threw his sixth no-hitter that year and won his 300th game. In 1989, at 42, he struck out more than 300 batters in a season for the sixth time. He has put the career strikeout record beyond the reach of mortal man, and it is continuing to grow, for 1991 is his 25th major-league season. After a quarter of a century in baseball, he pitched his seventh no-hitter May 1, 1991. Even the supposedly indestructible Johnson lasted only 21 years. The only major-league strikeout record that has thus far escaped him is Clemens' 20 Ks in a game. But Ryan has fanned 19 in a game four times. He set the single-season major-league strikeout record of 383 in 1973, the first year of the designated hitter in the American League, which means none of his victims was a pitcher. Koufax (382 strikeouts in 1965), Waddell (349 in 1904) and Feller (348 in 1946) had no such disadvantage. Can Ryan throw a lamb chop past a wolf? Can he make the ball disappear? Well, over the years, various mechanisms have been employed to time fastballs, all – until today's radar gun – with questionable accuracy. Experts pieced together picture frames to calculate Johnson's heater in excess of 100 miles per hour. Feller's fastball was clocked at 98.6 mph in a 1946 test conducted by the U.S. Army, using

Treasure Trove. *Collectibles, rarities, vintage photographs – seemingly all things bearing Nolan Ryan's name – are the desire of an army of collectors. This conglomera-tion features the collectibles of Coach Larry Cernoch, on loan for* NOLAN RYAN: The Authorized Pictorial History, *and the photographs of a lifetime.* (TRUITT ROGERS)

Could you throw in a Mickey Mantle?
Bryan Wrzesinski, 12, displays the 1968 Nolan Ryan "Rookie Card" he purchased for $12 in an Addison, Illinois, baseball card shop. Due to a clerical error, the shrewd collector received a $1,188 discount at the time of purchase. A court case ensued. The plaintiff and the defendant agreed to sell the card and donate the proceeds to charity.

a technique called "lumiline chronography." Twice in 1974, scientists from Rockwell International, utilizing the latest in radar technology, captured Ryan in actual games at more than 100 mph; the first time, at a peak of 100.9, occurred on August 20 against the Tigers, a game in which he threw seven pitches over 100 and 40 pitches better than 95 mph. And then, on August 20, they timed one of his pitches in the ninth inning at 100.8. The ninth inning! And this after he had already thrown 150 pitches. This would seem to confirm a suspicion held by timorous batters everywhere that the Ryan Express runs faster the later it gets. These times were recorded when Ryan was a young man, of course. But radar guns caught him at 99 mph in 1984 when he was 37 and at 98 a year later. In 1990, at an age when all previous fireballers had long since burned out, Ryan was still consistently clocked in the low to mid-90s. At 43, he was throwing the ball harder than youngsters

'Beaned' by Nolan. *The 5,000th strikeout went straight to the head of Darrel Johnson, a concessionaire at Arlington Stadium. "The Peanut Man," at right, poses with fan Buddy Goode, August 22, 1989.* (COURTESY JIM AND BOB MACDONALD)

half his age. Don't speak to me of legends.   There is simply no accounting for the phenomenon that is Nolan Ryan. He can't even explain it himself. The fact is, his arm is purely a wonder of nature, a miracle weapon, the strongest and the most durable in the history of baseball. If it weren't for the inconvenience it would surely impose on Nolan Ryan – when brushing his teeth, say, or pitching horseshoes – I'd propose that Ryan's arm be transported to the Hall of Fame the very day he retires, if, that is, he ever does retire. The Hall of Fame? Why not the Smithsonian, for it is indeed an American treasure. We can't do that, of course. But one thing is certain: His legend will survive as long as or longer than any of his mythic predecessors. All of them have probably gotten even faster with the telling and retelling of old tales.   That won't happen with Ryan. How fast, after all, can you get?

San Antonio artist Jim McKinnis hand-tinted this photograph as a tribute to Nolan. (COURTESY JIM MCKINNIS) . . . *And for the "baseball Bard Collector . . ." Fort Worth's annual Shakespeare In The Park poster features a likeness of William Shakespeare in a modern setting. The 1991 poster sported number 34.*
(CONCEPT AND DESIGN: GRAPHIC CONCEPTS GROUP/
ILLUSTRATION: JAMES TENNISON)

Jim Murray, Columnist, Los Angeles Times

HENRY AARON broke Babe Ruth's record. Pete Rose broke Ty Cobb's record.

But I have a feeling when they talk of the second half of the 20th century in baseball, the most frequently heard question by our generation will be "Did you ever see Nolan Ryan pitch?"

Nolan Ryan is a genuine American heirloom. Part pitcher, part legend. You get the feeling he was made up. No such person existed. He was a stereotype from a Frank Merriwell novel. The boy, upright, moral, modest, right off a Texas ranch with the gift of the gods – a 105-mile-an-hour fastball and a curve to match. (Burt L. Standish would have called it an "off-shoot.")

Nolan Ryan's pitches had so much stuff on them, no strike zone could hold them. It is the notion here that Nolan Ryan never really threw a ball as hard as he could have because it had to fit in that little keyhole baseball calls the strike zone.

I never saw Walter Johnson, but I find it hard to believe any human could ever throw a ball with the velocity and movement of a Nolan Ryan. Reggie Jackson gave the definitive description of trying to hit it. "Like trying to drink coffee with a fork," said Reggie.

There's no telling what records Nolan might have hung up had he played with – well, the Mantle-Maris Yankees, the Cincinnati Big Red Machine, the 1966-70 Baltimore Orioles.

Nolan never played on a team that would give him an eight-run lead. Nolan, like Sandy Koufax, threw a whole bunch of no-hit games because he had to. Anything less than a shutout and Nolan was out of there for a pinch hitter in the late innings.

You'd find it hard to make up a fictional character who led the world in strikeouts – also bases on balls. A pitcher who led the world in no-hit games – also wild pitches.

You know, baseball lore is funny. Every minor league in the country has a story of the young pitcher who threw the ball so hard it was invisible to the naked eye – only his control was so atrocious it didn't matter. What makes Nolan Ryan unique is, he was this mythical character who made good. He couldn't completely bottle this explosive force but he tamed it enough to be arguably (or, maybe, unarguably) the greatest pitcher who ever lived.

Pitching seven no-hit games, almost 18 years apart to the day, is a perfectly astonishing feat, but topping that with 12 one-hitters and a trunkful of two- and three-hitters...

It's rare that such enormous talent should be centered in so disciplined

PRECEDING PAGES: BRAD NEWTON. METS: SPORTS ILLUSTRATED; ANGELS: RONALD C. MODRA/SPORTS ILLUSTRATED

a person. Genius of any kind is often housed in such an unstable human being, it explodes all over the place and can be captured only in spurts.

Ryan was in possession of just such a torrent of transcendent ability that he could well have squandered it. Instead, he was always a model of discipline and reliability. You could always depend on Nolan,

if not his fastball, which often had a mind of its own. It was almost a living thing. Batters swore it wailed like a banshee on some nights.

No one ever had to go find Nolan Ryan in a bar. He never missed the team bus, a turn on the mound or an interview or photo session.

But he was hostage to his own brilliance. His pitches had so much movement on them they were, unlike their master, wickedly delinquent. You couldn't hit them, but some nights you didn't have to.

The baseball world was slow to catch on to the fact that there was a legend in its midst. The New York Mets thought he was going to be, of all things, a relief pitcher.

When he came to the Angels, he was prone to follow a night of pure incandescent pitching power with one in which the ball sailed out of the strike zone, to say nothing of the catcher's mitt, like a runaway space launch. No one ever knocked Nolan Ryan out of the box except Nolan Ryan. He pitched more 6- and 7-inning no-hitters than any pitcher who ever lived.

The situation got so frustrating that Angels General Manager Buzzie Bavasi, a front-office man from the old school, took to bitingly dismissing Nolan Ryan as "a guy I can replace with two .500 pitchers throwing 8-7."

Buzzie was missing the point, as he admits today. Nolan Ryan led the

so-so Angels to the playoffs in '79. He led the equally mediocre Houston Astros to the final four in '80, '81 and '86. Ryan was a winner. But Ryan's art transcended win-lose. He was a work of art on a mound. His arm should hang in the Louvre. His career should be encapsulated for future generations. What he did with a baseball, Rembrandt did with a brush,

Caruso with a high C. To have seen a Ryan fastball arcing past a wildly swinging Pete Rose or a Darryl Strawberry is to have seen baseball artistry at its most consummate. It's a part of Americana. And when future generations are asked if they saw Ryan pitch, the answer will come back, "Yeah, I saw Ryan pitch, and Astaire dance, and Hepburn act, and Crosby sing, and Louis fight and Aaron bat. I saw the best of my time."

ASTROS: JOHN G. ZIMMERMAN/SPORTS ILLUSTRATED; RANGERS: BRAD NEWTON

A special achievements class, the BRAVO Kids of David E. Smith Elementary in Birdville, I.S.D., Haltom City, Texas, likes a challenge. Their assignment in April 1991 was to write a Texas tall tale. They decided to write about Nolan Ryan, full-knowing it would be difficult to make up things that Nolan had not accomplished. They did their best and frankly, they did well. Here is an example . . .

When he was grown up, he was seven foot three inches tall and weighed 275 pounds. In 1965, he began playing professional baseball for the New York Mets.

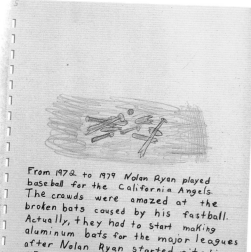

From 1972 to 1979 Nolan Ryan played baseball for the California Angels. The crowds were amazed at the broken bats caused by his fastball. Actually, they had to start making aluminum bats for the major leagues after Nolan Ryan started pitching. From 1980 to 1988 Nolan Ryan played for the Houston Astros Ryan continued to astonish everyone with his pitches. Some people were ready to put him out to pasture because of his age. They thought he was through.

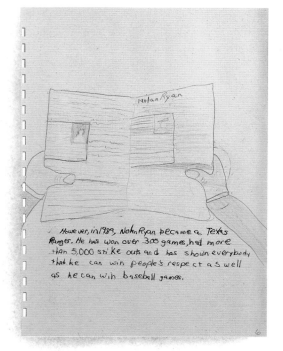

However, in 1989, Nolan Ryan became a Texas Ranger. He has won over 300 games, had more than 5,000 strike outs and has shown everybody that he can win people's respect as well as he can with baseball games.

BOUT NOLAN RYAN

.Wills   Illustrated by James D.Berry

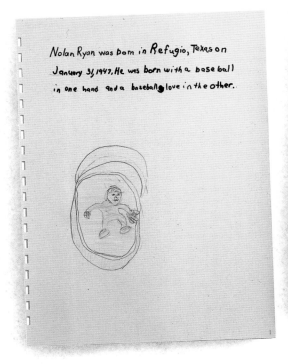

Nolan Ryan was Dom in Refugio, Texas on January 31, 1947. He was born with a baseball in one hand and a baseball glove in the other.

1

When Nolan Ryan was only five years old, he walked onto a baseball field where the Colt .45's were practicing. They asked him to leave, but he sat down on the pitcher's mound. They told him he could throw one pitch. Then, he must leave. He threw a fast pitch that went right over home plate, through the backstop, and into the concession stand. The pitch was so fast that the wind blew home base out of the ground and into the fence. That day, they wanted him to sign a contract to play

With the team but he had to finish school.

2

On his high school baseball team, he had a curve ball that was as wild as a Texas steer. In fact, some batters turned yellow as a sunflower just thinking about facing Ryan's pitches.

3

The baseball records Nolan Ryan has set can only be beaten by Nolan Ryan himself. Even in the nursing home Nolan Ryan will be continue to pitch.

7

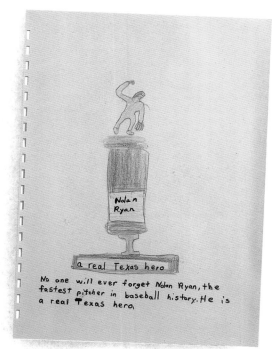

Nolan Ryan

a real Texas hero

No one will ever forget Nolan Ryan, the fastest pitcher in baseball history. He is a real Texas hero.

FOLLOWING PAGES: ARLINGTON STADIUM (COURTESY TEXAS RANGERS); GOODBYE (LINDA KAYE)

N   D   I   X

The 110 cards of the 1991 Nolan Ryan Texas Express Trading Card Series. (COURTESY PACIFIC TRADING CARD, INC.)

Tensions of a Pennant Race	Mets Clinch The N.L. East	"Keep the Ball Down"	A Playoff Victory for Ryan	A World Series Victory	The Amazin' Mets	Nolan Sets a Met Record for Strikeouts	One of the Worst Trades in Baseball
Looking Back on #1	No-Hitter #2	Single Season Strikeout Record	21 Wins in 1973	Fastest Pitch Ever Thrown Clocked at 100.9 MPH	No-Hitter #3	No-Hitter #4	Ryan & Tanana
A Ryan Home Run	The Fast Ball Grip	The Record 5th No-Hitter	No-Hitter #5	A Dream Fulfilled	Nolan passes Walter Johnson	Strikeout 4,000	Astros win the Western Division Title
A Real Special Moment	Nolan Enters the 1989 All-Star Game	Pitching in the 1989 All-Star Game	5,000 Strikeouts A Standing Ovation	Great Moments in 1989	Nolan and Dan Smith Rangers #1 Draft Pick	Ranger Club Record 16 Strikeouts	Last Pitch No-Hitter #6
11th Strikeout Title	232 Strikeouts in 1990	The 1990 Season		Pitcher Texas Rangers	1991: Nolan's 25th Season	Throwing Spirals	Running the Steps
The Spring Workout	Power versus Power	Awesome Power	Blazing Speed	The Pick Off	Nolan's A Real Gamer	Ranger Battery Mates	"The Glare"
Our Family of Five	Texas Beefmaster	The Gentleman Rancher	Texas Cowboy Life	The Ryan Family	Participating in a Cutting horse contest	Nolan Interviews	Lynn Nolan Ryan

205

YEAR	CLUB	W-L	ERA	G	GS	CG	SHO	SV	IP	H	R	ER	BB	SO
1965	Marion-1	3-6	4.38	13	12	2	1	0	78.0	61	47	38	56	115
1966	Greenville	*17-2	2.51	*29	28	9	5	0	183.0	109	59	51	*127	*272
	Williamsport	0-2	0.95	3	3	0	0	0	19.0	9	6	2	12	35
	New York (NL)	0-1	15.00	2	1	0	0	0	3.0	5	5	5	3	6
1967	Winter Haven-2	0-0	2.25	1	1	0	0	0	4.0	1	1	1	2	5
	Jacksonville	1-0	0.00	3	0	0	0	0	7.0	3	1	0	3	18
1968	New York (NL)	6-9	3.09	21	18	3	0	0	134.0	93	50	46	75	133
1969	New York (NL)	6-3	3.54	25	10	2	0	1	89.0	60	38	35	53	92
1970	New York (NL)	7-11	3.41	27	19	5	2	1	132.0	86	59	50	97	125
1971	New York (NL)-3	10-14	3.97	30	26	3	0	0	152.0	125	78	67	116	137
1972	California	19-16	2.28	39	39	20	*9	0	284.0	166	80	72	*157	*329
1973	California	21-16	2.87	41	39	26	4	1	326.0	238	113	104	*162	*383
1974	California	22-16	2.89	42	41	26	3	0	*333.0	221	127	107	*202	*367
1975	California	14-12	3.45	28	28	10	5	0	198.0	152	90	76	132	186
1976	California	17-*18	3.36	39	39	21	*7	0	284.0	193·	117	106	*183	*327
1977	California	19-16	2.77	37	37	#22	4	0	299.0	198	110	92	*204	*341
1978	California	10-13	3.71	31	31	14	3	0	235.0	183	106	97	*148	*260
1979	California-4	16-14	3.59	34	34	17	#5	0	223.0	169	104	89	114	*223
1980	Houston	11-10	3.35	35	35	4	2	0	234.0	205	100	87	*98	200
1981	Houston	11-5	*1.69	21	21	5	3	0	149.0	99	34	28	68	140
1982	Houston	16-12	3.16	35	35	10	3	0	250.1	196	100	88	*109	245
1983	Houston	14-9	2.98	29	29	5	2	0	196.1	134	74	65	101	183
1984	Houston	12-11	3.04	30	30	5	2	0	183.2	143	78	62	69	197
1985	Houston	10-12	3.80	35	35	4	0	0	232.0	205	108	98	95	209
1986	Houston	12-8	3.34	30	30	1	0	0	178.0	119	72	66	82	194
1987	Houston	8-16	*2.76	34	34	0	0	0	211.2	154	75	65	87	*270
1988	Houston-5	12-11	3.52	33	33	4	1	0	220.0	186	98	86	87	*228
1989	Texas	16-10	3.20	32	32	6	2	0	239.1	162	96	85	98	*301
1990	Texas	13-9	3.44	30	30	5	2	0	204.0	137	86	78	74	*232
	American League Totals	167-140	3.11	353	350	167	44	1	2625.1	1819	1029	906	1474	2949
	National League Totals	135-132	3.23	387	356	51	15	2	2365.0	1810	969	848	1140	2359
	Major-League Totals	302-272	3.16	740	706	218	59	3	4990.1	3629	1998	1754	2614	5308

*LED LEAGUE

Nolan was 19 years old when he joined the New York Mets in 1966.

SIGNING

1. Selected by New York Mets organization in June '65 free-agent draft (10th round, regular phase) . . . Signed by Red Murff on 6/26/65.
2. On military list, Jan. 3 - May 13, '67.
3. Acquired by California from New York Mets with pitcher Don Rose, catcher Francisco Estrada, and outfielder Leroy Stanton in deal for infielder Jim Fregosi on 12/10/71.
4. Granted free agency on 11/1/79 . . . Signed by Houston as a free agent on 11/19/79.
5. Granted free agency on 11/1/88 . . . Signed by Texas as a free agent on 12/7/88.

RYAN AS A RELIEVER

W-L	G	SV	IP	H	W	K	ERA
6-1	34	3	60.0	43	47	60	4.05

MAJOR-LEAGUE HITTING TOTALS

AVG	AB	H	HR	RBI
.110	852	94	2	33

STRIKEOUT HIGHS

19, 4 TIMES:	June 14, 1974 vs. Boston; August 12, 1974 vs. Boston; August 20, 1974 vs. Detroit; June 8, 1977 vs. Toronto.
18, ONCE:	September 10, 1976 at Chicago White Sox.
17, 3 TIMES:	September 30, 1972 vs. Minnesota; July 15, 1973 at Detroit; August 18, 1976 at Detroit.
16, 7 TIMES:	Latest on April 26, 1990 vs. Chicago.
15, 10 TIMES:	Latest on August 17, 1990 vs. Chicago.

NOLAN RYAN'S 48 MAJOR-LEAGUE RECORDS

STRIKEOUT RECORDS

1 Most Strikeouts, Major Leagues – 5308.
2 Most Strikeouts, Season, Major and American League – 383, California, 1973.
3 Most Strikeouts, Season, Major and American League, Right-handed Pitcher – 383, California, 1973.
4 Most Years, 100 or More Strikeouts, Major Leagues – 24, New York Mets, 1968, 1970, 1971; California, 1972-79; Houston, 1980-88; Texas, 1989-91 All-Star Break.
5 Most Consecutive Years, 100 or More Strikeouts – 22, New York Mets, 1970-71; California, 1972-79; Houston, 1980-88; Texas, 1989-91 All-Star Break.
6 Most Years, 200 or More Strikeouts, Major Leagues – 14, California, 1972-79, except 1975; Houston, 1980, 1982, 1985, 1987, 1988; Texas, 1989-90.
7 Most Years, 200 or More Strikeouts, American League – 9, California, 1972-79, except 1975; Texas, 1989-90.
8 Most Years, 300 or More Strikeouts, Major and American League – 6, California, 1972, 1973, 1974, 1976, 1977; Texas, 1989.
9 Most Strikeouts, Losing Pitcher, Extra-Inning Game, Major and American League – 19, California, August 20, 1974, 11 innings, lost 1-0.
10 Most Times, 15 or More Strikeouts, Major Leagues – 26, New York Mets, 1970 (1); 1971 (1); California, 1972 (4), 1973 (2), 1974 (6), 1976 (3), 1977 (2), 1978 (1), 1979 (1); Houston, 1987 (1); Texas, 1989 (1), 1990 (2), through 1991 All-Star Break (1).
11 Most Times, 15 or More Strikeouts, Game, American League – 23, California, 1972-79; Texas, 1989-91 All-Star Break.
12 Most Times, 10 or More Strikeouts, Game, Major Leagues – 211, 67 in National League, New York & Houston, 13 Years, 1966, 1968-71, 1980-88; 140 in American League; California and Texas, 10 Years, 1972-79, 1989-91 All-Star Break.
13 Most Times, 10 or More Strikeouts, Game, American League – 144, California and Texas, 10 Years, 1972-79, 1989-91 All-Star Break.
14 Most Times, 10 or More Strikeouts, Game, Season – 23, California, 1973.
15 Three Strikeouts, Inning, on Nine Pitched Balls* – New York Mets, April 19, 1968, 3rd inning; California, July 9, 1972, 2nd inning.
16 Most Consecutive Strikeouts, Game, American League – 8*, California, July 9, 1972; California, July 15, 1973.
17 Most Strikeouts, Two Consecutive Games, Major and American League – 32*, California, August 7 (13), August 12 (19), 1974, 17 Innings.
18 Most Strikeouts, Three Consecutive Games, Major and American League – 47, California, August 12 (19), August 16 (9), August 20 (19), 1974, 27.1 Innings.

NO-HIT AND LOW-HIT GAME RECORDS

19 Most No-Hitters Pitched, Major Leagues – 7, California, 1973 (2), 1974, 1975; Houston, 1981; Texas, 1990, 1991.
20 Most No-Hitters Pitched, American League – 6, California, 1973 (2), 1974, 1975; Texas, 1990, 1991.
21 Most No-Hitters Pitched, Season – 2*, California, May 15 and July 15, 1973.
22 Oldest Pitcher To Throw No-Hitter – 44 years, 3 months, at Arlington, Texas.

(continued)

23 Most Teams, Throwing No-Hitters – 3, California (4); Houston, Texas.
24 Most Different Decades, Throwing No-Hitters – 3, 1970s, 1980s, 1990s.
25 Longest Span Between Throwing No-Hitters – 8 years, 8 months, 16 days, September 26, 1981 until June 11, 1990.
26 Most Low-Hit (No-Hit and One-Hit) Games, Season, American League – 3*, California, 1973.
27 Most Low-Hit (No-Hit and One-Hit) Games, Career, Major League – 19.
28 Most One-Hit Games, Career, Major League – 12*.

BASES ON BALLS RECORDS

29 Most Bases on Balls, Major Leagues – 2617.
30 Most Years Leading Majors in Most Bases on Balls – 8, California, 1972, 1973, 1974, 1976, 1977, 1978; Houston, 1980, 1982.
31 Most Years Leading American League in Most Bases on Balls – 6, California, 1972, 1973, 1974, 1976, 1977, 1978.

MISCELLANEOUS RECORDS

32 Most Clubs Shut Out (Won or Tied), Season, Major and American League – 8*, California, 1972.
33 Most Years Leading Major Leagues in Wild Pitches – 6*, California, 1972, 1977, 1978; Houston, 1981, 1986; Texas, 1989.
34 Most Years Leading American League in Most Wild Pitches – 4, California, 1972, 1977, 1978; Texas, 1989.
35 Most Wild Pitches, Major Leagues – 257.
36 Most Years Leading American League in Most Errors, Pitcher – 4*, California, 1975, 1976, 1977 (tied), 1978.
37 Highest Strikeout Average Per Nine Innings, Season – 11.48, Houston, 1987, 270 Strikeouts, 211.2 Innings.
38 Highest Strikeout Average Per Nine Innings, Career – 9.57, 24 Seasons, 1966, 1968-90, 5308 Strikeouts, 4990.1 Innings.
39 Lowest Hits Allowed Average Per Nine Innings, Season – 5.26, California, 1972, 166 Hits, 284 Innings.
40 Lowest Hits Allowed Average Per Nine Innings, Career – 6.54, 24 Seasons, 1966, 1968-90, 3629 Hits, 4990.1 Innings.
41 Most Hits Allowed, Five Game Series, National League – 16, Houston, 1980.
42 Most Strikeouts, Total Series – 46*, New York Mets, 1969; California, 1979; Houston, 1980, 1986.
43 Most Strikeouts, Game Relief Pitcher – 7, New York Mets, October 6, 1969, Pitched Seven Innings.
44 Most Consecutive Strikeouts, Game – 4*, California, October 3, 1979.
45 Most Consecutive Strikeouts, Start of Game – 4*, California, October 3, 1979.
46 Highest Fielding Percentage, Pitcher, With Most Chances Accepted, Five Game Series, National League – 1.000*, Houston, 1980, Four Chances Accepted.
47 Most Assists, Pitcher, Five Game Series, National League – 3*, Houston, 1980.
48 Most Chances Accepted, Pitcher, Five Game Series, National League – 4*, Houston, 1980.

Ryan recorded his first major-league victory against the Houston Astros.

* TIES RECORD

DIVISIONAL SERIES RECORD

YEAR	CLUB	W-L	ERA	G	GS	CG	SHO	SV	IP	H	R	ER	BB	SO
1981	Houston vs. Los Angeles	1-1	1.80	2	2	1	0	0	15.0	6	4	3	3	14

CHAMPIONSHIP SERIES RECORD

YEAR	CLUB	W-L	ERA	G	GS	CG	SHO	SV	IP	H	R	ER	BB	SO
1969	New York vs. Atlanta	1-0	2.57	1	0	0	0	0	7.0	3	2	2	2	7
1979	California vs. Baltimore	0-0	1.29	1	1	0	0	0	7.0	4	3	1	3	8
1980	Houston vs. Philadelphia	0-0	5.40	2	2	0	0	0	13.1	16	8	8	3	14
1986	Houston vs. New York	0-1	3.86	2	2	0	0	0	14.0	9	6	6	1	17
League Championship Totals		1-1	3.70	6	5	0	0	0	41.1	32	19	17	9	46

WORLD SERIES RECORD

YEAR	CLUB	W-L	ERA	G	GS	CG	SHO	SV	IP	H	R	ER	BB	SO
1969	New York vs. Baltimore	0-0	0.00	1	0	0	0	1	2.1	1	0	0	2	3

ALL-STAR GAME RECORD

YEAR	CLUB	W-L	ERA	G	GS	CG	SHO	SV	IP	H	R	ER	BB	SO
1972	American League Atlanta			DID NOT PLAY										
1973	American League Kansas City	0-0	9.00	1	0	0	0	0	2.0	2	2	2	2	2
1975	American League Milwaukee			DID NOT PLAY										
1979	American League Seattle	0-0	13.50	1	1	0	0	0	2.0	5	3	3	1	2
1981	National League Cleveland	0-0	0.00	1	0	0	0	0	1.0	0	0	0	0	1
1985	National League Minnesota	0-0	0.00	1	0	0	0	0	3.0	2	0	0	2	2
1989	American League California	1-0	0.00	1	0	0	0	0	2.0	1	0	0	0	3
All-Star Game Totals		1-0	4.50	5	1	0	0	0	10.0	10	5	5	5	10

Named to 1977 A.L. squad to replace Frank Tanana, but declined.

On April 27, 1983, Ryan struck out his 3,509th victim, Montreal Expos player Brad Mills, lifting Ryan past Walter Johnson as the major league's all-time strikeout king.

AVERAGE PITCHING LINES

	TOTAL	IP	H	R	ER	W	K
All Starts	720	7	5	2	2	4	7
Wins as Starter	301	8	4	1	1	4	9
No Decision as ST	144	6	5	2	2	3	6
Losses as Starter	275	6	6	4	4	4	6

Per 9 Innings	TOTAL	H	W	SO	ERA		
All Starts	720	6.5	4.7	9.6	3.14		
Wins as Starter	301	4.9	4.0	9.8	1.43		
No Decision as ST	144	7.2	4.6	9.6	3.39		
Losses as Starter	275	8.5	5.7	9.3	5.51		

AVERAGE GAME SCORES

	TOTAL	RYAN'S TEAM	OPPONENT
All Starts	720	3.78	3.60
Wins as Starter	301	5.15	1.68
No Decision as ST	144	4.40	4.08
Losses as Starter	275	1.96	5.44

ALL-STAR GAME RECORD

YEAR	PCT.	G	PO	A	E	TC	DP
1966	1.000	2	1	0	0	1	0
1968	.800	21	5	11	4	20	0
1969	.800	25	0	4	1	5	0
1970	.840	27	11	10	4	25	2
1971	.870	30	5	15	3	23	2
1972	.854	39	7	28	6	41	2
1973	.949	41	10	27	2	39	1
1974	.909	42	12	48	6	66	1
1975	.811	28	12	18	7	37	3
1976	.873	39	14	34	7	55	1
1977	.873	37	20	35	8	63	1
1978	.852	31	13	33	8	54	3
1979	.902	34	8	29	4	41	1
1980	.889	35	13	27	5	45	0
1981	.955	21	5	16	1	22	3
1982	.955	35	9	33	2	44	1
1983	.941	29	4	28	2	34	0
1984	.900	30	7	11	2	20	0
1985	.929	35	6	20	2	28	0
1986	.931	30	10	17	2	29	2
1987	.967	34	11	18	1	30	1
1988	.867	33	8	18	4	30	0
1989	.909	32	11	19	3	33	0
1990	1.000	30	7	13	0	20	1
TOTALS	**.896**	**740**	**209**	**512**	**84**	**805**	**25**

STRIKEOUTS

1	Nolan Ryan	5308
2	Steve Carlton	4136
3	Tom Seaver	3640
4	Bert Blyleven	3631
5	Don Sutton	3574
6	Gaylord Perry	3534
7	Walter Johnson	3508
8	Phil Niekro	3342
9	Ferguson Jenkins	3192
10	Bob Gibson	3117

EARNED RUN AVERAGE

	(3000 or more ip)	
1	Walter Johnson	2.37
2	Grover Alexander	2.56
3	Whitey Ford	2.74
4	Tom Seaver	2.86
5	Jim Palmer	2.86
6	Stan Covaleski	2.88
7	Juan Marichal	2.89
8	Wilbur Cooper	2.89
9	Bob Gibson	2.91
10	Carl Mays	2.92
11	Don Drysdale	2.95
12	Carl Hubbell	2.98
13	Lefty Grove	3.06
14	Warren Spahn	3.08
15	Gaylord Perry	3.10
16	Urban Faber	3.1475
17	Eppa Rixey	3.1497
18	Nolan Ryan	3.16

INNINGS PITCHED

1	Cy Young	7377
2	Pud Galvin	5959
3	Walter Johnson	5923
4	Phil Niekro	5404

(continued)

5	Gaylord Perry	5352
6	Don Sutton	5281
7	Warren Spahn	5244
8	Steve Carlton	5216
9	Grover Alexander	5189
10	Kid Nichols	5089
11	Tim Keefe	5072
12	Nolan Ryan	4990.1

GAMES STARTED

1	Cy Young	818
2	Don Sutton	756
3	Phil Niekro	716
4	Steve Carlton	709
5	Nolan Ryan	706
6	Tommy John	700
7	Gaylord Perry	690
8	Pud Galvin	682
9	Walter Johnson	666
10	Warren Spahn	665

SHUTOUTS

1	Walter Johnson	110
2	Grover Alexander	90
3	Christy Mathewson	83
4	Cy Young	77
5	Eddie Plank	64
6	Warren Spahn	63
7	Mordecai Brown	63
8	Tom Seaver	61
9	Bert Blyleven	60
10	Nolan Ryan	59

VICTORIES

1	Cy Young	511
2	Walter Johnson	416
3	Christy Mathewson	373
4	Grover Alexander	373

(continued)

5	Warren Spahn	363
6	Pud Galvin	361
7	Kid Nichols	361
8	Tim Keefe	342
9	Steve Carlton	329
10	John Clarkson	327
11	Don Sutton	324
12	Phil Niekro	318
13	Gaylord Perry	314
14	Tom Seaver	311
15	Charles Radbourn	308
16	Mickey Welch	307
17	Eddie Plank	305
18	Nolan Ryan	302
19	Lefty Grove	300
20	Early Wynn	300

FEWEST HITS PER 9 INNINGS, CAREER

	(Minimum 2000 Innings)	
1	Nolan Ryan	6.54
2	Sandy Koufax	6.79
3	Andy Messersmith	6.94

(continued)

4	Hoyt Wilhelm	7.02
5	Sam McDowell	7.03

FEWEST HITS PER 9 INNINGS, SEASON

1	Nolan Ryan	1972	5.26
2	Luis Tiant	1968	5.30
3	Carl Lundgren	1907	5.63

STRIKEOUT LEADERS AVERAGE PER 9 INNINGS

	(1500 or more ip)	SO	IP	AVG.
1	Nolan Ryan	5308	4990.1	9.57
2	Sandy Koufax	2396	2325.0	9.27
3	Sam McDowell	2453	2492	8.86
4	Roger Clemens	1424	1513	8.47
5	Dwight Gooden	1391	1523.2	8.22
6	Mark Langston	1448	1597.1	8.16
7	Bob Gibson	3117	3885.0	7.22
8	Steve Carlton	4136	5216.0	7.14
9	Mickey Lolich	2832	3640	7.00
10	Tom Seaver	3640	4781.1	6.85

Ryan became the first pitcher who failed to win the Cy Young Award after leading the league in strikeouts (270) and earned run average (2.76) in 1987. His record was 8-16.

RYAN'S MILESTONE VICTORIES

NO.	DATE	OPPONENT	SCORE	OPPOSING PITCHER	NOTES
1	April 14, 1968	Houston	4-0	Larry Dierker	6.2 sho ip
50	April 11, 1973	Minnesota	4-1	Bill Hands	cg
100	June 1, 1975	Baltimore	1-0	Ross Grimsley	4th no-hitter
150	September 24, 1978	Chicago (AL)	7-3	Francisco Barrios	—
200	July 27, 1982	Cincinnati	3-2	Charlie Leibrandt	cg
250	August 27, 1986	Chicago (NL)	7-1	Jamie Moyer	6 sho ip
300	July 31, 1990	Milwaukee	11-3	Chris Bosio	7.2 ip

Eddie Matthews of the Atlanta Braves became Ryan's first major-league strikeout victim on September 11, 1966.

MAY 15, 1973, AT KANSAS CITY
CALIFORNIA 3, KANSAS CITY 0

NOLAN RYAN chalked up the first of his major-league record four no-hitters for the California Angels as he stopped the Kansas City Royals for the first hitless game by an Angels right-hander in the club's history. Ryan finished with 12 strikeouts as he recorded at least one whiff in every inning except the fifth. The only close call of the game came in the eighth inning when Royals pinch hitter Gail Hopkins hit a looping liner into left field which shortstop Rudy Meoli came up with on a running over-the-shoulder catch with his back to the plate. The Angels and Ryan got all the offensive support they needed from right fielder Bob Oliver, two of the three RBIs with a solo home run and a single.

| California | 200 | 001 | 000 | — | 3 | 11 | 0 |
| Kansas City | 000 | 000 | 000 | — | 0 | 0 | 0 |

Ryan and Torborg. Dal Canton, Garber (6) and Taylor, Kirkpatrick, WP-Ryan (5-3) LP-Dal Canton (2-2).

Ryan Pitching Line: 9 IP   0 H   0 R   0 ER   3 BB   12 SO

JULY 15, 1973, AT DETROIT
CALIFORNIA 6, DETROIT 0

THE "EASIEST" NO-HITTER for Ryan in terms of scores as he turned in his second no-hitter of the 1973 campaign, again on the road, by stopping the Detroit Tigers 6-0. Ryan had 17 strikeouts for the game with 16 of them coming in the first seven innings. However, his arm stiffened up somewhat in the top of the eighth as the Angels batted around while scoring five runs to break open a close game. Ryan had to rely on no special defensive accomplishments to preserve the no-hitter as he became the fifth man in history to throw two no-hitters in a season.

| California | 001 | 000 | 050 | — | 6 | 9 | 0 |
| Detroit | 000 | 000 | 000 | — | 0 | 0 | 0 |

Ryan and Kusnyer. J. Perry, Scherman (8), Farmer (8) and Sims. WP-Ryan (11-11). LP-J. Perry (9-9).

Ryan Pitching Line: 9 IP   0 H   0 R   0 ER   4 BB   17 SO

SEPTEMBER 28, 1974, AT ANAHEIM
CALIFORNIA 4, MINNESOTA 0

NOLAN RYAN makes the most of his final start of the 1974 campaign by ringing up his third career no-hitter to raise his final record to 22-16 at the expense of the Minnesota Twins, 4-0. Ryan started in splendid fashion as his first seven pitches were strikes, but he also had to contend with no less than eight walks – seven of them in the first five innings. The Angels won it with two runs in both the third and fourth innings with center fielder Morris Nettles driving home three of them.

| Minnesota | 000 | 000 | 000 | — | 0 | 0 | 2 |
| California | 002 | 200 | 00x | — | 4 | 7 | 0 |

Decker, Butler (3) and Borgmann. Ryan and Egan. WP-Ryan (22-16). LP-Decker (16-14).

Ryan Pitching Line: 9 IP   0 H   0 R   0 ER   8 BB   15 SO

JUNE 1, 1975, AT ANAHEIM
CALIFORNIA 1, BALTIMORE 0

NOLAN RYAN moved into a tie with Dodgers great Sandy Koufax as he fired the fourth no-hitter of his career in nipping the Baltimore Orioles 1-0. Making his 12th start of the season, Ryan polished off the Orioles with nine strikeouts as he came up with his fourth no-hit effort in a period of 109 starts. The only offensive output in the game came in the bottom of the third when Angels third baseman Dave Chalk singled home Mickey Rivers.

| Baltimore | 000 | 000 | 000 | — | 0 | 0 | 0 |
| California | 001 | 000 | 000 | — | 1 | 9 | 1 |

Grimsley, Garland (4) and Hendricks. Ryan and Rodriguez. WP-Ryan (9-3). LP Grimsley (1-7).

Ryan Pitching Line   9 IP   0 H   0 R   0 ER   4 BB   9 SO

On July 15, 1973, Ryan set the major-league record for strikeouts in a no-hitter with 17 against Detroit.

SEPTEMBER 26, 1981, AT HOUSTON
HOUSTON 5, LOS ANGELES 0

HISTORY WAS MADE when Nolan Ryan became the first man in the history of baseball to pitch five no-hitters in his career as he notched a crucial 5-0 win over the Los Angeles Dodgers. In winning, Ryan wound up with 11 strikeouts (the 135th time in his career that he fanned 10 or more men in a game) while walking only three. He threw a total of 129 pitches (52 balls, 77 strikes). Ryan stood at 10 strikeouts through the opening six innings, but set down only one more the rest of the way as he retired the final 19 batters in a row. Catcher Alan Ashby gave the Astros a 2-0 lead with a two-run single in the third and then Houston wrapped up the win with three more tallies in the eighth.

| Los Angeles | 000 | 000 | 000 | — | 0 | 0 | 1 |
| Houston | 002 | 000 | 03x | — | 5 | 11 | 0 |

Power, Goltz (4), Forster (5), Stewart (8), Howe (8), and Scioscia. Ryan and Ashby. WP-Ryan (10-5), LP-Power (1-3).

Ryan Pitching Line: 9 IP   0 H   0 R   0 ER 3 BB   11 SO

JUNE 11, 1990, AT OAKLAND
TEXAS 5, OAKLAND 0

NOLAN RYAN accomplished several milestones with the sixth no-hitter of his major-league career. At the age of 43 years, 4 months, 12 days, he became the oldest pitcher to ever throw a no-hitter while also becoming the first to reach that achievement in three different decades and with three different teams. Ryan was making just his second start since coming off the disabled list and was still bothered by the lower back trouble that had benched him for nearly three weeks. He allowed only two baserunners, walks to Walt Weiss in the third and Mike Gallego in the sixth, while fanning 14 and throwing 132 pitches. The Rangers offense was provided by a pair of 2-run homers by Julio Franco and a solo blast by John Russell, who was catching Ryan for the first time.

| Texas | 210 | 020 | 000 | — | 5 | 9 | 0 |
| Oakland | 000 | 000 | 000 | — | 0 | 0 | 0 |

Ryan and Russell. Sanderson, Norris (7), Nelson (9), and Quirk, Steinbach (9). WP-Ryan (5-3), LP-Sanderson (7-3).

Ryan Pitching Line: 9 IP   0 H   0 R   0 ER 2 BB   14 SO

MAY 1, 1991, AT ARLINGTON
TEXAS 3, TORONTO 0

NOLAN RYAN pitched after only four days rest to allow him the opportunity to pitch in front of the home crowd on Arlington Appreciation Night. Ryan started out strong, striking out 13 of the first 21 batters, and finished the game with 16 strikeouts. Ryan allowed only two base runners on walks. All three Rangers runs were scored in the bottom of the third, with Ruben Sierra providing the offensive output on a two-run homer. It is interesting to note that Roberto Alomar was the final out of the game; his father, Sandy Alomar, was Ryan's second baseman in his first two no-hitters.

| Toronto | 000 | 000 | 000 | — | 5 | 9 | 0 |
| Texas | 003 | 000 | 00x | — | 3 | 8 | 1 |

Ryan and Stanley. Key, MacDonald (7) and Fraser (8). WP-Ryan (3-2), LP Key (4-1).

Ryan Pitching Line: 9 IP   0 H   0 R   0 ER 2 BB   16 SO

RYAN'S NO-HITTERS
ENDED IN THE NINTH INNING

DATE	OPPONENT	PLACE	BATTER	HIT	FINAL SCORE
Aug. 7, 1974	Chicago (A.L.)	Chicago	Dick Allen	1 out single	L, 1-2
July 13, 1979	New York (A.L.)	Anaheim	Reggie Jackson	1 out single	W, 6-1
Apr. 27, 1988	Philadelphia	Houston	Mike Schmidt	1 out single	ND in 3-2 win
Apr. 23, 1989	Toronto	Toronto	Nelson Liriano	1 out triple	W, 4-1
Aug. 10, 1989	Detroit	Arlington	Dave Bergman	1 out single	W, 4-1

RYAN'S MILESTONE STRIKEOUTS

NO.	DATE	OPPONENT	PLAYER
1	Sep.11, 1966	Atlanta	Pat Jarvis
100	June 18, 1968	Houston	Denny LeMaster
500	April 18, 1972	Minnesota	Charlie Manuel
1000	July 3, 1973	Oakland	Sal Bando
1500	August 25, 1974	New York (AL)	Sandy Alomar
2000	August 31, 1976	Detroit	Ron LeFlore
2500	August 12, 1978	Cleveland	Buddy Bell
3000	July 4, 1980	Cincinnati	Cesar Geronimo
3500	April 17, 1983	Montreal	Andre Dawson
3509*	April 27, 1983	Montreal	Brad Mills
4000	July 11, 1985	New York (NL)	Danny Heep
4500	Sep. 9, 1987	San Francisco	Mike Aldrete
5000	Aug. 22, 1989	Oakland	Rickey Henderson

*BREAKS WALTER JOHNSON'S ALL-TIME STRIKEOUT RECORD

STRIKEOUT LEADERS BY AGE

AGE	1ST	2ND	3RD
25	329 NOLAN RYAN	291 Roger Clemens	283 McDowell-Seaver
26	383 NOLAN RYAN	301 Rube Waddell	289 Tom Seaver
27	367 NOLAN RYAN	347 Rube Waddell	348 Bob Feller
28	303 J.R. Richard	286 Rube Waddell	271 Mickey Lolich
29	382 Sandy Koufax	327 NOLAN RYAN	313 J.R. Richard
30	341 NOLAN RYAN	317 Sandy Koufax	308 Mickey Lolich
31	303 Mike Scott	260 NOLAN RYAN	254 Ed Walsh
32	268 Bob Gibson	233 Mike Scott	225 Toothpick Jones
33	269 Bob Gibson	268 Jim Bunning	262 Dazzy Vance
34	274 Bob Gibson	252 Jim Bunning	238 Gaylord Perry
35	286 Steve Carlton	253 Jim Bunning	245 NOLAN RYAN
36	232 Gaylord Perry	208 Bob Gibson	196 Bert Blyleven
37	286 Steve Carlton	203 Cy Young	200 Dazzy Vance
38	275 Steve Carlton	225 Bert Blyleven	209 NOLAN RYAN
39	248 Phil Niekro	223 Charlie Hough	194 NOLAN RYAN
40	270 NOLAN RYAN	208 Phil Niekro	174 Charlie Hough
41	228 NOLAN RYAN	176 Phil Niekro	150 Cy Young
42	301 NOLAN RYAN	114 Charlie Hough	109 Cy Young
43	232 NOLAN RYAN	144 Phil Niekro	116 Gaylord Perry

BROTHER STRIKEOUT VICTIMS

Sandy Jr. and Roberto Alomar

Felipe, Jesus and Matty Alou

George and Ken Brett

Ollie and Oscar Brown

Jose and Hector Cruz

Tony and Chris Gwynn

Dane and Garth Iorg

Eddie and Rich Murray

Graig and Jim Nettles

Joe and Phil Niekro

Cal and Bill Ripken

STRIKEOUT LEADERS AVERAGE PER 9 INNINGS

	(1500 or more ip)	SO	IP	AVG.
1	Nolan Ryan	5308	4990.1	9.57
2	Sandy Koufax	2396	2325.0	9.27
3	Sam McDowell	2453	2492.0	8.86
4	Roger Clemens	1424	1513.0	8.47
5	Dwight Gooden	1391	1523.2	8.22
6	Mark Langston	1448	1597.1	8.16
7	Bob Gibson	3117	3885.0	7.22
8	Steve Carlton	4136	5216.0	7.14
9	Mickey Lolich	2832	3640.0	7.00
10	Tom Seaver	3640	4781.1	6.85

FATHER/SON STRIKEOUT VICTIMS

Sandy Sr. and Roberto, Sandy Jr. Alomar

Bobby and Barry Bonds

Tito and Terry Francona

Ken and Ken Griffey

Dick and Dick Schofield

Maury and Bump Wills

MOST VALUABLE PLAYER STRIKEOUT VICTIMS

Hank Aaron	Barry Bonds
Ernie Banks	Roger Maris
Maury Wills	Brooks Robinson
Roberto Clemente	Zoilo Versalles
Orlando Cepada	Carl Yastrzemski
Bob Gibson	Harmon Killebrew
Willie McCovey	Boog Powell
Johnny Bench	Vida Blue
Joe Torre	Dick Allen
Pete Rose	Reggie Jackson
Steve Garvey	Jeff Burroughs
Joe Morgan	Fred Lynn
George Foster	Thurman Munson
Dave Parker	Rod Carew
Keith Hernandez	Jim Rice
Willie Stargell	Don Baylor
Mike Schmidt	George Brett
Dale Murphy	Robin Yount
Ryne Sandberg	Cal Ripken
Willie McGee	Don Mattingly
Andre Dawson	George Bell
Kirk Gibson	Jose Canseco
Kevin Mitchell	Rickey Henderson

CAREER VICTORIES VERSUS EACH TEAM

Royals	23
White Sox	20
Twins	19
Cubs	16
Padres	15
Tigers	15
Braves	13
Giants	13
Reds	13
Dodgers	12
Expos	12
Pirates	12
Yankees	12
Brewers	12
Indians	12
A's	11
Rangers	11
Cardinals	10
Mariners	10
Phillies	9
Red Sox	8
Mets	7
Blue Jays	6
Orioles	5
Angels	3
Astros	3

RYAN'S MANAGERS

NEW YORK METS
1968-'71 Gil Hodges
CALIFORNIA ANGELS
1972 Del Rice
1973 Bobby Winkles
1974 Bobby Winkles/ Dick Williams
1975 Dick Williams
1976 Dick Williams/ Norm Sherry
1977 Norm Sherry
1978-'79 Jim Fregosi
HOUSTON ASTROS
1980-'81 Bill Virdon
1982 Bill Virdon/ Bob Lillis
1983-'85 Bob Lillis
1986-'88 Hal Lanier
TEXAS RANGERS
1989-'91 Bobby Valentine

Ryan suffered from dyslexia as a child.

10 OR MORE STRIKEOUT GAMES

YEAR	10	11	12	13	14	15	16	17	18	19	TOTAL	IP	SO	AVG. 9 INNS
1966	-	-	-	-	-	-	-	-	-	-	0	3.0	6	18.00
1968	1	1	1	-	1	-	-	-	-	-	4	134.0	133	8.93
1969	1	1	-	-	-	-	-	-	-	-	2	89.0	92	9.30
1970	1	1	-	2	-	1	-	-	-	-	5	132.0	125	8.52
1971	1	-	1	-	-	-	1	-	-	-	3	152.0	137	8.11
1972	6	4	1	-	2	1	2	1	-	-	17	284.0	329	10.43
1973	5	3	8	4	1	-	1	1	-	-	23	326.0	383	10.57
1974	3	2	1	1	-	3	-	-	-	3	13	333.0	367	9.92
1975	2	-	2	-	-	-	-	-	-	-	4	198.0	186	8.45
1976	2	4	3	-	1	1	-	1	1	-	13	284.0	327	10.36
1977	4	5	6	2	1	1	-	-	-	1	20	299.0	341	10.26
1978	4	2	3	4	-	1	-	-	-	-	14	235.0	260	9.96
1979	5	1	3	-	-	1	-	-	-	-	10	223.0	223	9.00
1980	2	1	-	-	-	-	-	-	-	-	3	234.0	200	7.69
1981	2	2	-	-	-	-	-	-	-	-	4	149.0	140	8.46
1982	5	4	-	1	-	-	-	-	-	-	10	250.1	245	8.81
1983	2	2	2	-	-	-	-	-	-	-	6	196.1	183	8.40
1984	-	3	1	-	-	-	-	-	-	-	4	183.2	197	9.64
1985	2	1	-	-	-	-	-	-	-	-	3	232.0	209	8.11
1986	2	-	-	1	1	-	-	-	-	-	4	178.0	194	9.81
1987	4	5	2	-	-	-	1	-	-	-	12	211.2	270	11.48
1988	2	4	-	1	-	-	-	-	-	-	7	220.0	228	9.33
1989	4	6	2	4	1	1	-	-	-	-	18	239.1	301	11.32
1990	-	4	1	-	1	1	1	-	-	-	8	204.0	232	10.24
TOTALS	**60**	**56**	**37**	**20**	**9**	**10**	**7**	**3**	**1**	**4**	**207**	**4990.1**	**5308**	**9.57**

TOP SEASONAL STRIKEOUT TOTALS

NAME	L/R	TEAM	YEAR	G	SO	IP	AVG. 9 INNS
Nolan Ryan	R	California (A)	1973	41	383	326	10.57
Sandy Koufax	L	Los Angeles (N)	1965	43	382	336	10.23
Nolan Ryan	R	California (A)	1974	42	367	333	9.92
Rube Waddell	L	Philadelphia (A)	1904	46	349	384	8.18
Bob Feller	R	Cleveland (A)	1946	48	348	371	8.44
Nolan Ryan	R	California (A)	1977	37	341	299	10.26
Nolan Ryan	R	California (A)	1972	39	329	284	10.43
Nolan Ryan	R	California (A)	1976	39	327	284	10.36
Sam McDowell	L	Cleveland (A)	1965	42	325	273	10.71
Sandy Koufax	L	Los Angeles (N)	1966	41	317	323	8.83
Walter Johnson	R	Washington (A)	1910	45	313	373	7.55
J.R. Richard	R	Houston (N)	1979	38	313	292	9.65
Steve Carlton	L	Philadelphia (N)	1972	210	310	293.1	9.52
Mickey Lolich	L	Detroit (A)	1971	45	308	376	7.37
Mike Scott	R	Houston (N)	1986	37	306	275.1	10.01
Sam McDowell	L	Cleveland (A)	1970	39	304	305	8.97
Walter Johnson	R	Washington (A)	1912	50	303	368	7.41
J.R. Richard	R	Houston (N)	1978	36	303	275	9.92
Rube Waddell	L	Philadelphia (L)	1903	39	302	324	8.39
Vida Blue	L	Oakland (A)	1971	39	301	312	8.68
Nolan Ryan	R	Texas (A)	1989	32	301	239.1	11.32

TOP SEASONAL STRIKEOUT TOTALS

YEAR-BY-YEAR STRIKEOUTS, EACH TEAM

NATIONAL LEAGUE

	1966	1968	1969	1970	1971	1980	1981	1982	1983	1984	1985	1986	1987	1988	TOTALS
Atlanta	3	14	0	6	14	13	12	26	17	11	28	20	14	22	200
Chicago	-	1	5	29	15	8	11	14	2	20	16	10	19	35	185
Cincinnati	-	21	11	7	5	14	34	41	8	27	23	21	29	33	274
Houston	3	26	7	14	11	-	-	-	-	-	-	-	-	-	61
Los Angeles	-	20	2	10	13	38	11	23	20	18	9	14	48	29	255
Montreal	-	0	23	1	16	26	15	17	19	7	22	29	9	7	191
New York	-	-	-	-	-	5	17	30	29	22	11	24	2	12	152
Philadelphia	-	17	21	28	9	16	12	8	9	16	26	20	27	24	233
Pittsburgh	-	5	11	12	13	10	1	19	10	25	14	12	20	12	233
San Diego	-	-	-	1	21	25	9	26	33	14	39	13	21	14	216
San Francisco	-	7	1	17	0	23	12	21	31	17	11	25	61	32	258
St. Louis	-	22	11	0	20	22	6	20	5	20	10	6	20	8	170
TOTALS	**6**	**133**	**92**	**125**	**137**	**200**	**140**	**245**	**183**	**197**	**209**	**194**	**270**	**228**	**2359**

AMERICAN LEAGUE

	1972	1973	1974	1975	1976	1977	1978	1979	1989	1990	TOTALS
Baltimore	14	29	18	21	43	24	11	8	28	0	196
Boston	29	39	53	7	34	21	18	13	29	19	253
California	-	-	-	-	-	-	-	-	44	22	66
Chicago	36	35	48	21	48	20	32	19	16	41	316
Cleveland	21	14	23	12	19	27	27	6	14	15	178
Detroit	29	44	36	0	27	23	11	18	21	15	234
Kansas City	25	46	58	14	38	31	18	36	41	9	316
Milwaukee	30	21	31	33	9	0	11	22	28	19	204
New York	3	26	14	21	9	22	8	18	11	22	154
Oakland	56	31	18	14	49	26	21	17	13	33	278
Seattle	-	-	-	-	-	36	38	13	29	25	141
Texas	43	33	23	26	10	29	9	20	-	-	193
Toronto	-	-	-	-	-	44	24	13	26	9	116
TOTALS	**329**	**383**	**367**	**186**	**327**	**341**	**260**	**223**	**301**	**232**	**2949**

19 OR MORE STRIKEOUTS IN ONE GAME

K	PITCHER	DATE	IP
19	Charlie Sweeney	6-07-1884	9
19	Hugh Daily	7-07-1884	9
21	Tom Cheney	9-12-1962	16
19	Luis Tiant	7-03-1968	10
19	Steve Carlton	9-15-1969	9
19	Tom Seaver	4-22-1970	9
19	Nolan Ryan	6-14-1974	13
19	Nolan Ryan	8-12-1974	9
19	Nolan Ryan	8-20-1974	11
19	Nolan Ryan	6-08-1977	10
20	Roger Clemens	4-29-1986	9

Prior to the 1991 season, Claudell Washington had been Ryan's most frequent strikeout victim, going down 39 times.

NOLAN RYAN, GREATEST STRIKEOUT PITCHER IN THE WORLD

MASAICHI KANEDA is considered to be the greatest pitcher in the history of the Japanese leagues. In a 20-year career (1950-1969) Kaneda struck out 4,490 batters, and upon his retirement he had nearly 1,000 more strikeouts than anyone in the history of the game. On September 8, 1987, Nolan Ryan passed Masaichi Kaneda to become the international strikeout king.

RYAN SETS RECORD, STRIKES OUT 19 BATTERS FOUR TIMES

NO OTHER PITCHER in baseball history has struck out 19 batters more than once in their career; Ryan did it three times in one season (1974). Ryan did it a fourth time in 1977, striking out 19 Blue Jays in 10 innings.

Ryan's record of 211 games of 10 or more strikeouts is better than double that of anyone else. Sandy Koufax is the closest with 97.

The 1991 season was Ryan's 25th year in the major-leagues. Deacon McGuire and Tommy John are the only two with more (26 years each).

Jennifer Briggs

Jennifer Briggs is an 11-year veteran and a feature writer for the *Fort Worth Star-Telegram*. Briggs has covered high school, college and professional sports. In 1986, she won an *Associated Press* Sports Editors honor for her investigative sports reporting.

Briggs grew up in Arlington, Texas, spending summers in the stands of Arlington Stadium. Her formal association with baseball began at age 18 when she joined the Texas Rangers as a bat girl. Briggs covered the Rangers for *The Associated Press* in 1984 and 1985.

Ron Fimrite

Ron Fimrite covered 16 years of professional baseball, including the World Series, for *Sports Illustrated*, starting in 1971. Since 1986 he has concentrated on features and profiles for the magazine, including a 1986 article on Nolan Ryan. He is *SI*'s book critic and has authored two books of his own: *Way to Go* and *The Square*.

Kenny Hand

Kenny Hand is a sports columnist for *The Houston Post*, and covered the Houston Astros from 1977 to 1985 for the daily.

In 1990, Hand received first place in column writing by the Texas *Associated Press* Sports Editors.

Prior to working for *The Houston Post*, Hand worked for the *Dallas Times-Herald* and was the sports editor of the *(Arlington) Citizen-Journal*.

Marcy Kornreich

Marcy Kornreich is a Boston-based writer specializing in business, marketing and advertising. She has served as the managing editor of *Adweek/New England* and previously worked with several national and regional publications published for high-tech marketers, college bookstore owners, health-club operators and military commissary managers.

Tracy Ringolsby

Tracy Ringolsby is a former president of the Baseball Writers Association of America. He has covered the Texas Rangers for *The Dallas Morning News* since 1986. He is the national baseball writer for the paper. Ringolsby first wrote of Nolan Ryan early in his career, as a California Angels beat reporter for *The (Long Beach) Independent Press-Telegram* from 1977 to 1979.

Peter Schmuck

Sportswriter Peter Schmuck was in his rookie year as a baseball beat writer when Nolan Ryan helped lead the California Angels to their first division title in 1979. Ryan left the club after that season, but Schmuck remained to cover the Angels in 1980 and again from 1984-1989 for the *Orange County Register*.

He also covered the Los Angeles Dodgers (1981-1983) and currently is the Baltimore Orioles beat writer for *The Baltimore Sun*. Schmuck has won numerous awards during his fifteen years of journalism.

Mark Schramm

Mark Schramm is director of sports for National Public Radio in Washington, D.C. He has been with NPR since 1983 and has worked as a reporter, editor and producer for NPR's "Morning Edition," covering the arts, science and sports. His greatest professional joy comes from working with the legendary Red Barber and with Bob Edwards, the host of "Morning Edition."

Schramm remains a steadfast "Washington Senators" fan, twenty years after the team moved to Texas.

Bill Shaikin

Bill Shaikin covers the California Angels for *The (Riverside) Press-Enterprise*. He previously covered the Oakland Athletics and San Francisco Giants for *United Press International*. He is the author of *Sport and Politics: The Olympics and the Los Angeles Games*. The *Associated Press* Sports Editors honored Shaikin in their 1991 competition. He graduated from the University of California at Berkeley, where he served two years as the play-by-play voice for the college's baseball team.

Ron Kroichick

Ron Kroichick is a senior writer at *The Sacramento Bee*. He has covered the Oakland A's beat since 1990. Additionally, Kroichick has covered the World Series, two All-Star games, the American League Playoffs and the College World Series. He is also a regular contributor to *SPORT* magazine.

Jim Murray

Jim Murray is a Pulitzer-Prize-winning writer for the *Los Angeles Times*, where he began in 1961. In 1990, he was honored with the Pulitzer Prize for commentary and was inducted into the Baseball Hall of Fame in Cooperstown, New York. Murray also was awarded his 15th National Association of Sportscasters and Sportswriters Award in 1990.

Murray is the author of three books: *The Best of Jim Murray*, *The Sporting World of Jim Murray* and *The Murray Collection*.

John D. Rawlings

John D. Rawlings is the editor of *The Sporting News*. He became editor of the weekly in 1990. Previously, Rawlings served as a journalism instructor at the University of Missouri, a copy editor for the sports desk and national desk of *The Miami Herald* and an assistant sports editor with *The Philadelphia Inquirer*. He also was the executive sports editor of the *San Jose Mercury News*.

Rawlings has been a member of *The Associated Press* Sports Editors since 1983 and served as the organization's president for 1990-91.

Jim Reeves

Jim Reeves has been with the *Fort Worth Star-Telegram* for 22 years. Eleven years of his career have been devoted to covering the Texas Rangers, longer than any other reporter in the Rangers' history.

In 1989, Reeves was awarded the Texas *Associated Press* Managing Editors Association Award for "Best Spot News Story" for his coverage of Nolan Ryan's 5,000th strikeout. In 1990, he won a Katie Award and a Texas *Associated Press* Managing Editors Association Award for "Best Columnist in Texas."

Arnie Stapleton

Arnie Stapleton joined *The Associated Press* in 1988. Prior to serving the *AP*, Stapleton was a writer for the *Dallas Times-Herald* and *The San Antonio Light*. Stapleton played baseball for New Mexico Highlands University, where he was a right-handed pitcher and played first base.

Larry Swindell

Larry Nolan Swindell has been a professional journalist for more than thirty years. He affiliated with the *Fort Worth Star-Telegram* in 1980 as its books editor and critic-at-large. Swindell has authored five biographies of bygone motion picture personalities – Spencer Tracy, John Garfield, Carole Lombard, Gary Cooper and Charles Boyer.

Swindell also serves as the vice president and publications director of the Fort Worth-Dallas chapter of the Society for American Baseball Research.

Craig R. Wright

Craig R. Wright is a sabermetric consultant to several major-league clubs, including the Los Angeles Dodgers, Texas Rangers and Oakland Athletics. He also serves as director of major-league operations with STATS Inc. of Chicago. He researches and writes the radio show "A Page from Baseball's Past" (1985-1991).

Wright served as essay editor for *The Great American Baseball Stat Book* and has written numerous articles on baseball, as well as two books: *The Man Who Stole First Base* and *The Diamond Appraised*.

ACKNOWLEDGMENTS

The concept was simple: create and craft a hardbound pictorial history of Nolan Ryan for his fans with the same standard of excellence he set for his life – at home and on the field. The execution of such grand vision was not as simple.

The vision was kept alive by the determination of The Summit Group's President Clark Kemble and Vice President Brent Lockhart, for without their invaluable effort, there would be no *NOLAN RYAN: The Authorized Pictorial History*. No less instrumental in the formative stages was legal counsel Jim Anderson and Nolan's agent Matt Merola.

An all-star line up of talent collaborated to assure the quality standard set forth in the beginning. Deep appreciation goes to award-winning photographer Truitt Rogers for hours spent in his studio and in Alvin, Kent Pingel for editorial direction and captions, designer Cheryl Corbitt and assistant Carter Montsinger for their countless hours of nurturing this project, and designer Gary Templin for the creation of the "Great Moments" logo.

Relentless editing and proofing were provided by Louie Hulme, Mark Witherspoon, Tommy Thomason, Mercedes Olivera, Erika Paige Brockhouse, Clinton Batte, Ida Gonzalez, Tom Gostkowski, Denise Graham, Renee Rounsaville, Troy B.

Reese, and Alleen and Tommie Whiteley.

A very gracious thanks goes to Coach Larry Cernoch. His supply of Nolan Ryan collectibles was invaluable.

Many thanks to the hundreds of researchers who provided photographs and data for this publication, like Gail Henry, Mike Dickson, and Sunny Smith, all from *Sports Illustrated*; Liam Thorpe; Joe Nick Patoski from *Texas Monthly*; private collector, Bob Rook; Kerri McCarthy of *The Associated Press*; Darby Harper of *United Press International*; Rich Pilling of *The Sporting News*; Lisa Skolnick; and Brad Newton, Texas Rangers photographer.

Thanks also go to: Larry and Ingrid Holdorff, Mary Lou Williams, Harry and Kim Spilman, Thomas McReynolds, Tim Meade, Rob Matwick, Don Jeffries, Aubrey Horner, Mark Schramm, Madonna Ballard, Monica Chapman, Rae Randall and *The Fort Worth Star Telegram's* Jim Reeves.

Though it is extraneous to mention our gratitude toward Nolan and Ruth Ryan, we would like to offer them our humble appreciation. As Nolan has played baseball for many decades to the fans' delight, this book will remain forever as a symbol of the legendary Nolan Ryan.

It is our aspiration that this book will remain on your shelf for as long as Nolan remains in your heart.

THE SUMMIT GROUP